HELP WANTED

The Complete Guide to Human Resources for Canadian Entrepreneurs

Also available in the series from

The Magazine for Canadian Entrepreneurs

PROFIT: The Magazine for Canadian Entrepreneurs

Beyond the Banks: Creative Financing for Canadian Entrepreneurs,
by Allan Riding and Barbara Orser (ISBN: 0-471-64208-8)

Secrets of Success from Canada's Fastest-Growing Companies,
by Rick Spence (ISBN: 0-471-64233-9)

*Make it Legal: What Every Canadian Entrepreneur Needs to Know about the
Law,* by Margaret Kerr and JoAnn Kurtz (ISBN: 0-471-64245-2)

*Marketing Masters: The Best Ideas, Tips & Strategies From Canada's Savviest
Marketeers,* edited by Ian Portsmouth (ISBN: 0-471-64274-6)

HELP WANTED

The Complete Guide to Human Resources for Canadian Entrepreneurs

BY MARGARET BUTTERISS

JOHN WILEY & SONS CANADA, LTD

Toronto • New York • Chichester • Weinheim • Brisbane • Singapore

John Wiley & Sons Canada, Ltd
22 Worcester Road
Etobicoke, Ontario
M9W 1L1

Canadian Cataloguing in Publication Data

Butteriss, Margaret
    Help wanted: the complete guide to human resources for Canadian entrepreneurs

Includes bibliographical references and index.
ISBN 0-471-64388-2

1. Personnel management — Canada.   I. Title.

HF5549.2.C3B87 1999   658.3'00971   C99-930903-X

Production Credits
Cover & text design: Interrobang Graphic Design Inc.
Printer: Tri-Graphic Printing

Printed in Canada
10 9 8 7 6 5 4 3 2 1

CONTENTS

ACKNOWLEDGEMENTS: BUSINESS PEOPLE ON THE FRONT LINES

In preparing this book, I interviewed a number of owners and managers of small and medium-size enterprises, along with members of organizations that offer various types of services and support to such enterprises. These people graciously gave me their time in order to provide me with stories and information to support the various chapters in the book. Through them, I was able to illustrate the new HR methods and procedures with a number of up-to-date examples from small businesses that are succeeding in the contemporary economy. My thanks go to all of these people, whose anecdotes and ideas you will meet as you read on.

THE ENTREPRENEURS

David Anderson, Executive Vice-President, CANATOM NPM, Montreal and Oakville

CANATOM NPM, which operates in the nuclear industry, provides two types of service to clients. The first is the building of new plants. The second is support: operations, maintenance, in-service inspection, radioactive materials management, and waste management.

CANATOM NPM was formed in 1967 and is now owned by AGRA Industries, SNC Lavalin, and BFC Construction Corporation. Outside of Canada, its principal markets are in Asia, North and South America, Europe, and the former Soviet Union. It has 320 full-time employees, primarily engineers and technicians who can apply their specialty to the nuclear environment. Projects are staffed by contractors, part-time employees, and individuals who have formed their own companies and contract their services to CANATOM NPM.

Karen Flavelle, President, Purdy's Chocolates, Vancouver

Purdy's Chocolates is a family-owned business that manufactures and sells chocolates, roasted nuts, and ice cream. The company has retail stores in major malls in British Columbia and Alberta. It employs about 600 people, 120 of whom work on the manufacturing side. Since the business is highly seasonal, it uses full-time, part-time, and casual employees. Karen took over as president in 1996, while her father moved into semi-retirement taking on the role of chairman.

David Haslam, President, Presidential Plumbing Ltd., Etobicoke, Ontario

The company, established by David in 1991, was Number 28 on "The 1998 PROFIT 100" survey of Canada's fastest-growing companies. It supplies and installs plumbing products for residential and commercial properties within the greater Toronto area and employs 30 people.

Mabel Jakimtschuk, Owner, Sherwood Village Spa, Mississauga, Ontario

Sherwood Village Spa provides aesthetic services for skin and body care. The company was started in 1989 by Mabel and another partner; in 1994 the original owner sold her share of the business to Mabel and her sister. The spa has grown rapidly: in its early years it employed five aestheticians who each saw about five clients per day. It has recently moved to a 2,000-square-foot facility and now employs eight aestheticians who each have ten to 12 clients daily.

David Marshall, President, Ergonomic Accessories Inc., Concord, Ontario

Ergonomic Accessories Inc. was Number 35 on "The 1998 PROFIT 100 List." In 1989 David and his father founded the company of which he owns 90 per cent. The other 10 per cent is held by the warehouse manager. The company is a wholesale distributor of ergonomically designed office furniture and accessories to office furniture retailers and contract office dealers. It employs trained ergonomic consultants who advise companies on these products. The company employs six persons full-time and uses self-employed agents who represent various furniture products and who are paid by commission only.

Susan Niczowski, President, Summer Fresh Salads Inc., Woodbridge, Ontario

The company was Number 41 on "The 1998 PROFIT 100 List." Susan and her mother started it in 1991 in the kitchen of their home. At first they made upscale gourmet potato, macaroni, and pasta salads with longer shelf lives than other products in this range. In the first year of operation, the company sold to specialty stores and in the second year began selling to larger retailers. By 1995 growth required a move to an 18,000-square-foot facility that was recently expanded to 25,000 square feet. Summer Fresh Salads Inc., which now employs 86 people, had 1998 revenues of $12 million.

Kieran O'Briain, President, Kee Transport, Mississauga, Ontario

The company was Number 14 on "The 1998 PROFIT 100 List." Founded by Kieran in 1987, Kee Transport supplies trucking companies with drivers and today has offices in Montreal, Mississauga, Winnipeg, Calgary, Edmonton, and Vancouver. It employs about 250 full-time drivers and 12 full-time administrative staff. Ninety-eight per cent of sales are to trucking companies that haul freight across North America and to private companies that have their own trucking operations.

THE BUSINESS EXPERTS

Lynne Allen, Acting Manager, Ontario Ministry of Economic Development, Trade and Tourism

The Ministry of Economic Development, Trade and Tourism organized a conference for innovative fast-growing firms. Entitled The Wisdom Exchange: Accelerating Growth through Innovation, the meeting was held in May 1998; Lynne provided me with insights from the discussion groups which was very helpful in the preparation of Chapter 2, "Attracting and Retaining the Right People."

Joan Berta, President, CAFE: The Canadian Association of Family Enterprises

One of the prime areas of focus for CAFE is helping family-owned businesses deal with the problem of succession. Joan provided information on a variety of CAFE programs, including Personal Advisory Groups (discussed in Chapter 17) and succession issues for family-owned enterprises (Chapter 18).

Lynda Bowles, FCA, Partner, Deloitte and Touche LLP

Lynda is a partner in the Audit Practice of Deloitte and Touche. One of her areas of expertise is the high-growth sector, which covers companies of all sizes that are going through significant growth. She has been in public accounting since 1979 and is an active member of numerous not-for-profit organizations. She was awarded the 1998 Metro Toronto YWCA Woman of Distinction Award in the business category.

David Howe, Partner, Eckler Partners Ltd.

Eckler Partners is the largest Canadian-owned independent actuarial and consulting firm, with offices in all major Canadian centres. It has evolved into an integrated consulting firm specializing in a full range of actuarial services, including all aspects of pension and benefits, such as plan design, administration, systems, legislative compliance, risk and funding analysis, and negotiation and review of insurance contracts. David provided information on employee benefits (Chapter 10).

Jonathan Kovacheff, Ph.D., President, Kovacheff Consulting Group Inc.

Jonathan's consulting practice covers corporate governance, leadership development, strategic human resources management, and strategy development. He has consulted with over 75 corporations in both public and private sectors. He specializes in providing assistance to the financial services sector but also consults to a number of fast-growing entrepreneurial companies.

Jonathan has practised law and taught human resources and organization behaviour at the University of Western Ontario. He provided information on setting up advisory boards (Chapter 17) and dealing with succession questions (Chapter 18) in small and medium-size organizations.

Ellie Maggio, Principal, William M. Mercer Limited

As a senior consultant and principal with William M. Mercer Limited's Human Resource and Compensation Management Practice, Ellie Maggio provides consulting assistance to private and public sector organizations in a variety of sectors. She has been with the company since 1989, and prior to that, she worked as a consultant at a strategic management consulting firm in the financial services industry. In addition, she has served in a research capacity on several public sector contracts with the Ontario Legislative Assembly and Revenue Canada.

Ellie is also the Regional Vice-President, Ontario West, of the Canadian Compensation Association (CCA), a planning committee member of the Canadian Human Resource Planners (CHRP), and an adviser to *HR Reporter*. She is a publishing author in the HR field and speaks regularly at human resources and compensation management conferences. She has an honours BA in Public Policy and Administration from York University.

Rick Spence, Publisher and Editor, PROFIT, The Magazine for Canadian Entrepreneurs

Rick gave me names and facts of the people behind the companies on "The 1998 PROFIT 100 List" of fast-growing companies and pointed me to various articles the magazine has published on people management for growth-oriented small and medium-size enterprises. He is the author of *Secrets of Success from Canada's Fastest-Growing Companies*, one of the books in the PROFIT series published by John Wiley and Sons.

Anne Sutherland, Senior Vice-President, Small and Medium Enterprises, Royal Bank of Canada

Royal Bank is Canada's leading and largest supplier of financial services to small and medium enterprises (SMEs). Anne provided me with a summary of the common financial issues facing the owners and managers of SMEs, particularly as they relate to the HR and organizational aspects of the business. She also supplied me with a number of relevant publications produced by the Royal Bank which are referred to in this book.

Others

There are other people I would also like to acknowledge for the assistance they gave me in producing this book. Ruth Weaver and Janet Vasey shared some of their insights with me in terms of both working for, and being, small business entrepreneurs. Penny Hozy and Kiem Lan Njoo helped me with the writing and editing of first drafts. My greatest thanks go to Theresa Moritz. She assisted me in making the chapters that I had written or drafted more interesting and readable, and I owe an enormous debt to her.

My thanks go to Karen Milner and Elizabeth McCurdy of John Wiley and Sons Canada, Ltd for encouraging me to write this book. Finally my thanks go to my husband Brian and my sons Robin and Jeremy for supporting me yet again, through the production of another book.

INTRODUCTION

Equipped with technical and business expertise, entrepreneurs often expect these skills to be enough to develop a company. They do not foresee that a developing business will bring with it new responsibilities, in particular, the management of a growing workforce.

Many small and medium-size Canadian businesses compete effectively and prosper mainly because of the skills and knowledge of their employees. Currently the fastest-growing businesses are in such fields as biotechnology and software design, and these companies depend on their employees to develop innovative products and services.

Thus, the management of people—the human resources (HR) function—is critical if a business is to survive and stay ahead of the competition.

This book is written for the owners of small and medium-size businesses, entrepreneurs who frequently perform the human resources function themselves and want help with it. These owners are likely to be faced with the following HR issues:

- creating a vision, culture, and leadership style that motivates employees
- developing compensation tools that attract and retain employees, particularly in markets where some skills are in short supply
- ensuring that recruitment and selection techniques attract people with the competencies that will help the company survive and grow
- developing performance management processes that ensure that both the company goals and the individual development of people are accomplished
- establishing a few key policies that ensure fairness and consistency across the organization
- making use of advisers and consultants where appropriate

A CASE IN POINT

The following case illustrates how some of these issues can arise. As I began to write this book, I was asked by a small high-tech company to review both its organizational structure and its HR processes, practices, and policies. In terms of profit and of size, this company was rapidly moving from small to medium-size status.

The Company

The company provides professional services for a specific computer software application: it sells licences, provides implementation and support, and trains personnel to use the software. It also has a placement business that provides contract staffing to third-party organizations.

The company had recently been bought from its original owners and was in the process of consolidating its various functions and services and of expanding its market base into a much larger geographic area. It employs about 50 full-time employees and has numerous people on contract.

Many of the people in the company have been with it for less than a year; a few have been there since it was founded four years ago. Most people in the company liked working in it because of the growth potential and the challenge it provided.

Organizational Concerns

The review I conducted showed that there were a number of concerns facing the company:

- The owner and the management team had differing visions of the company and of the business plan for the next two years.

- Roles and responsibilities were unclear because the company had grown rapidly, causing job and organization design to change frequently.

- The company had a very competent board of directors, but it was not being used effectively to provide advice to the business.

- Decision-making meetings, both for the management team and for all employees, were too few and far between.

Clearly, growth had brought this company to a critical point: a lack of sufficient integration among the owners, board of directors, management, and employees was emerging as a potential barrier to further expansion.

Human Resources Concerns

My review also identified a number of significant HR problems facing the company:

- Salaries and hourly rates were not consistent across the company, even when people were doing the same job. Vacation policies also differed from person to person. This inconsistency in compensation was due to the fact that no policy had been established with regard to levels of compensation and benefits for similar functions and jobs in the company.

- Recruitment processes were not clearly defined and this was causing numerous delays in hiring people. Since the company was hiring in a very competitive labour market, potential candidates were being lost to competitors.

- There were few documented processes for such things as performance evaluation, discipline, termination, relocation policy, and salary administration.

My review showed that the company needed to make several crucial improvements in HR. First, the management team had to define and agree upon its human resources goals and procedures. Once this was done, the employees needed to be integrated through two basic methods:

1. A policy manual was needed to allow all employees to clearly understand their compensation (salaries, wages, rates, benefits, etc.) and to understand the company's HR policies as a whole. This was especially important because the company's full-time employees and contract people were spread all over the country.

2. An orientation program was required to ensure that all employees heard the same message about the company, understood its culture, and were clear on its policies and processes.

Does this all sound familiar? It probably does, particularly for those companies which, like the one I reviewed, are growing rapidly and are finding that people and organizational issues are taking up much of their time.

HUMAN RESOURCES:
A CHALLENGE FOR THE GROWING COMPANY

In this brief case history, it is important to note that the organizational and the human resources problems were intimately linked, and that it would be very hard to improve one without improving the other. The close connection of human resources with strategic planning and management is a basic fact about HR in the modern economy.

The fact that good HR practices are necessary to create a vital company, and that HR can play a strategic as well as transactional role was a chief topic of my book, *Re-inventing HR: Changing Roles to Create the High-Performance Organization* (John Wiley and Sons Canada, Ltd, 1998). That book focused on large, established national or international organizations. But it is equally true that smaller companies seeking to grow and be successful must hire, motivate, develop, and retain people who can help them face the challenges of the business and the market place. This book is a guide for small businesses on the management of people. Its emphasis is practical. Its first function is to provide a complete map for developing an adequate and flexible HR function for the growing company. This map will allow owners and managers who must perform the HR function themselves, to do so successfully in a way that adds value. Along the way, the book also provides ideas and theories about how the new HR methods can assist ownership and management at the strategic level.

OVERVIEW OF THE BOOK

The book covers the entire spectrum of the HR function for small and medium-size companies in five parts.

Part One: HR Basics for Small Business

Chapter 1, "HR Insights on Leadership," presents the key characteristics of effective leadership, particularly as the entrepreneur assumes greater responsibility for a growing staff. Chapter 2, "Attracting and Retaining the Right People," gives a comprehensive introduction to HR's most crucial task, hiring and integrating employees into an organization.

Part Two: The Recruitment Process

The five chapters of this section (Chapters 3 through 7) expand on Chapter 2 with a complete guide to "attracting the right people," the first part of the crucial HR task. Chapter 3, "Creating an HR Plan," details all that needs to occur on the management side before effective hiring and employee relations can begin. Chapter 4, "Job Descriptions and Competency Profiles," covers the process and procedures for defining the positions the company requires. Competencies are the skills and knowledge required to perform the job to the required standards. Chapter 5, "Sources of Candidates," looks at where to find suitable people to fill vacancies. Chapter 6, "The Interview," looks at the questions you should ask in the interview and the stages of the interview process. Chapter 7, "Reference Checks and the Offer Letter," discusses the need to check candidates' references and what needs to be covered in the letter offering the successful individual the job.

Part Three: Compensation

These four chapters (Chapters 8 to 11) discuss the full range of questions about compensation, from what to pay your employees to how to pay them. Chapter 8, "Pay: Who Gets What?" lets business owners know what to consider in deciding what to pay a person who joins the company. Chapter 9, "Incentives," outlines the growing importance of providing incentives to support wages and salaries. Chapter 10, "Benefits," covers the different types of benefits, such as medical and dental, that a company might consider providing for its employees. Chapter 11, "Payroll Processes," considers how to put employees on the payroll and the processes used to pay people.

Part Four: Development

"Integrating and Retaining the Right People" is the focus of this section. Today, HR is often called upon for improved contributions in its traditional area of expertise, dealing with people. This is the subject of Chapters 12 through 15, "Good Communications and New Employee Orientation," "Performance Reviews," "Training and Development," and "Problem Employees: Performance Improvement." Chapter 16, "Termination Procedures," provides procedures for what to do when someone quits or you have to fire an employee. This is a subject that entrepreneurs consistently identify as the HR issue which gives them the most difficulty.

Part Five: Special Issues

We have left to a separate part three special situations facing the small business operator. Chapter 17, "Advisory Boards," discusses the growing practice among entrepreneurs of organizing mentors, outside experts, and others into a panel of advisers to provide advice on the development of the business. Chapter 18, "Planning for Management Succession," offers methods—often neglected in single-owner, family-owned, and other small companies—for providing for a successor and preparing for transition. Chapter 19, "Hiring a Consultant," tells how to recognize when the HR function has outgrown the capacities of the management team to handle it in-house, and how to acquire competent help with this problem.

HR BASICS FOR SMALL BUSINESS

Energy, enthusiasm, and a good idea are not sufficient to ensure business success. While survivorship and growth may reflect certain factors external to the firm, the most important ingredient both to business success and to access to capital are the management competencies in the business: the firm's managerial capacity.[1]

—Allan Riding and Barbara Orser

It's a thought likely to bring many entrepreneurs up short, that their success hinges not only on their willingness to work harder than others or to think better than others, but also on their ability to work with others, especially to manage others. And yet I've seen it time and time again: a business reaches an exciting growth spurt and then founders. When I'm called in for a consultation, I find that the owner or operator has not spent enough time on the company's growing workforce.

Chapter 1, "HR Insights on Leadership," considers the key components of leadership and the way an entrepreneur can demonstrate this in the organization. Chapter 2, "Attracting and

Retaining the Right People," concerns the ways that can be used to attract people to work in smaller, entrepreneurial organizations. It also looks at how to retain employees once they have been hired.

HR INSIGHTS ON LEADERSHIP

Human resources theory and practice has a lot to offer the entrepreneur intent on keeping a new business alive and growing. The first and most fundamental insight is that entrepreneurs must provide leadership. Leadership in setting and meeting goals for particular tasks is part and parcel of starting a business, of course, but a growing business requires other types of leadership as well. Many entrepreneurs recognize that to be successful they have to be good at managing not only the technical aspects of their business but also the people side. Still, they often underestimate the effort that will be required in this area.

In this chapter we will look at six activities that are most frequently identified with good people management:

- Motivating Employees: The Entrepreneur as Role Model
- Providing a Clear Vision and Direction
- Coordinating the Organization's Structure, Vision, and Direction
- Communicating Clearly and Sharing Information
- Delegating Effectively

• Building an Effective Team—Hiring and Firing

An entrepreneur with a growing business probably already possesses some of these qualities, for example, the ability to provide a role model of achievement, and only needs encouragement to cultivate them fully. However, other activities on the list, such as the ability to delegate, may be new skills. It must be emphasized that the entire skill set is crucial to integrating the best HR practices into a growing business.

MOTIVATING EMPLOYEES: THE ENTREPRENEUR AS ROLE MODEL

Entrepreneurs believe in themselves—that's as basic to being an entrepreneur as is the ability to set task goals. It is not surprising, then, that many entrepreneurs recognize instinctively that their own example of energy, commitment, and hard work is the best thing they have to offer their employees. They truly believe they must "walk the talk," and so they are likely to recognize, even before they begin to cultivate people management skills, that they possess the key leadership quality of being able to motivate employees by their example. It was a theme sounded over and over in the interviews I conducted with entrepreneurs: they were still comparatively new to studying human resources theory, but they did think of themselves as role models. Following are some brief examples.

Kieran O'Briain of Kee Transport: "Leadership through example is the biggest thing with me. I have a head coach philosophy about leadership. My people operate with their basic instincts, and I'll lend assistance where needed and as needed."

Susan Niczowski of Summer Fresh Salads Inc.: "Basically, I want people in the organization to use me as their role model. I've had various mentors that I've followed, and I want my people to have respect and follow me in my path."

Karen Flavelle of Purdy's Chocolates: "I think part of the loyalty to Purdy's is the result of people being encouraged by me and the whole management team to go beyond what they thought they could do and enjoyed the satisfaction of that."

Most people agreed that the fundamental aspect of leadership was the importance of leading by example. Attitude was identified as something to be shared. The next step is to ensure that these shared attitudes are contributing to the business because they are being directed along a shared path. Entrepreneurs are as likely to have a vision of their future success as they are to have a strong work ethic. The effective leader works to articulate this vision clearly and set a clear direction for achieving it.

PROVIDING A CLEAR VISION AND DIRECTION

People management calls for the entrepreneur to develop and communicate a clear vision and direction of the company to all employees. Vision may seem too fanciful a word to use in the hard-headed world of business, but it's actually as practical as setting a timetable and knowing your destination when you start a trip. According to Joanne Thomas Yaccato, visions "are nothing more than dreams with a time limit. When you are starting out on a journey, it helps to know the destination. Your end point is simply where you want to end up eventually. If you don't have a very clear idea of what your goals and vision are, the end point becomes a moving target."[2]

David Haslam agrees. "You have to have a vision," he told me. "You have to talk about the future. People want to know that you want to grow and not just remain the same. People don't like to think that they're always going to remain in the same place. I think it's just human nature that people always want to try to do something better, and to be part of an organization that can promote and creates confidence. And I think good leadership will create confidence.

"When you're the leader you have to be able to make decisions, whether they're right or wrong. You like to think they're the right decisions, but you have to make them. I think poor leadership comes when people ask questions and get maybes, or there are variances, and they're unsure of things. People lose faith in leadership when you cannot make a clear decision."

An entrepreneur who communicates a vision for the business helps current employees understand where the company is headed and allows prospective employees to decide whether or not their personal goals align well with those of the business. But it's also good for the leader to articulate that vision, since it creates a baseline against which all future decisions can be measured.

Providing a clear direction is David Anderson's leadership style at CANATOM NPM. "One thing I've found very useful is to ensure that the company and the individual set goals and objectives. I talk about SMART objectives: **S**pecific, **M**easurable, **A**ttainable **R**each in **T**ime. I always ask people to set objectives. And I find that if you can really get people to think about those things at day one, and put it in their own words, they come through."

How Do You Create a Vision and Direction?

There are many ways for a business operator to develop a vision and direction for the organization. The one I have used frequently and successfully with organizations of all sizes encourages the leader of the company, often with the total management team, to picture the company in the future and then to identify ways and means of making that picture come true. Although the goal is a "vision," the method is practical: I use a specific time line in the relatively near future, say two years, and focus the questions on the key business areas of company offerings, whether products or services, and on markets.

In some cases, management has involved the whole employee population in developing the vision and direction; such involvement certainly promotes general commitment to a new program. More than one meeting with employees may be necessary to ensure that everyone has a chance for input. However, at the end of the day, the management team has to decide what the vision and direction is.

Below is a summary of the questions I have used in helping business operators develop vision and direction for their organizations.

VISION

1. What will our company look like in two years in terms of:
   - products and services offered?
   - geographical and demographic markets served?

2. What will the company's stakeholders be saying about the company in two years? The stakeholders considered might include:
   - customers
   - strategic partners
   - employees
   - shareholders
   - vendors

3. What will the culture and values of the company be in two years? Participants should be encouraged to describe all aspects of the workplace and the company culture.
   - What will it be like to work here? Will we be working in teams with a high degree of authority, or will we create a workplace that is led by the owner/manager/buyer?
   - Will we encourage flexibility in working hours and a creative way of thinking?
   - What will our values be in the sense that they guide the way we work. For instance, will we operate under such values as:
     —honesty
     —focus of the customer
     —partnership with employees

DIRECTION

The vision that emerges from this process of discussion becomes the basis for setting a company direction: in David Anderson's terms, setting goals and objectives. The questions here are deceptively simple.

1. Where are we now?

2. What will help us to achieve our vision within the next two years?

3. What might hinder us from achieving the vision?

The answers to these questions provide the groundwork for the next step, which is to coordinate both company structure and operating procedures with the new vision and direction. The effective leader recognizes that such coordination is key to growth; more will be said about these questions in the section below entitled "Recovering a Sense of Direction."

According to Karen Flavelle of Purdy's Chocolates, her role is "making sure the company is running the way it needs to, doing the right things on a day-to-day basis, and ensuring that the building blocks, or the bench strengths, are in place. The retail team has evolved and has become much more cohesive under a strong leader. The finance and administration team also has a strong leader who is moving that department forward. The goal is to get that bench strength to a point where we can branch off from it confidently, go beyond it and have a vision of where we want to head next."

COORDINATING THE ORGANIZATION'S STRUCTURE, VISION, AND DIRECTION

When an enterprise starts up, the owner and the few employees that have come on board do everything. They instinctively know who has to do what, and who is responsible for a particular area. However, as the company grows, the notion of "everyone doing everything" can lead to problems. The organization will need more specialization, but each specialization will mean a team of experts seeking its own identity and yet needing to be integrated into the organization as a whole.

An entrepreneur can recognize when an organization is getting into trouble. Here are some of the symptoms to watch for:

• duplication of effort

• things not getting done

• grumbling

• territorial disputes

• loss of productivity, efficiency, and effectiveness

The effective leader takes action quickly when signs of trouble appear. I have facilitated many sessions and undertaken numerous organization reviews with the goal of integrating a business's organization and rules with its goals for growth. Below is a short overview of the process I have followed for sorting out structures, roles, and responsibilities.

Recovering a Sense of Direction

Essentially, the process begins with a review of vision and direction along the lines set out in the previous section; that is, a target is set for performance over the next two years, and a program for achieving the target is defined. When a company first develops a plan for the future (as described in the box above entitled "Direction"), three questions are asked:

1. Where are we now?

2. What will help us to achieve our vision within the next two years?

3. What might hinder us from achieving the vision?

In the discussion that follows, suggestions are given on how to develop meaningful responses to each of these important questions.

Where Are We Now?

An organization with growing pains should begin with a thorough assessment of current operations, both structure and employee assignments. For example: A small but growing company in the financial services industry conducted a review of its operations just to see whether it matched the existing business direction. Each of the senior managers in the team defined what they did, what their roles were in relation to marketing, sales, distribution, and all the financial and administrative aspects of the company. They were then able to see, as they grew, what was being done and not being done in the company that was making them vulnerable in terms of providing client satisfaction.

As a result of these meetings, they were able to do a slight restructuring of the organization to combine various departments, and they were also able to clearly define the role of each of the departments and the people in them. As a result, customer satisfaction improved by about 10 per cent, and profitability increased also, so it proved well worth the two or three days in total that it took to do the review.

The review was conducted with the help of an outside HR facilitator who was able to ensure that people addressed all the difficult issues and that it didn't turn into a "bitching and whining" session, but remained very constructive and focused on the needs of the business.

What Will Help Us Achieve Our Vision?

After each key member has described his or her role, other members of the team should be consulted on what changes they would like to see. The consultation should be far-reaching, encouraging suggestions both for ending as well as starting particular practices. Such consultation ensures that everyone's expectations about the person or role are clear.

Next, new job descriptions should be written that incorporate both employee suggestions and any relevant feedback on organizational structure from customers or suppliers. These new job descriptions which emerge should be reviewed in light of the company's two-year vision and direction program. The following questions should be asked:

- Will the proposed changes help to ensure that the vision for the next two years is achieved?

- Are new hires necessary?

- Is reorganization and regrouping necessary in light of new definitions of roles and responsibilities?

What Might Hinder Us from Achieving Our Vision?

The final step is documentation of the new organization structure and of the new employee roles and responsibilities. This information should be shared with all employees and with customers and suppliers where appropriate.

The questions to ask in relation to what stops the company from achieving its vision and business plans are:

• Can we compete effectively with our competition?

• Do we have the right people with the right skills to achieve our vision and plan over the next two to three years?

• Do we have the necessary financing in place, and if not, how will we find it?

• Do we have the appropriate suppliers and strategic partners?

• Do we have the appropriate distribution channels?

• Are our marketing plans clearly defined and have we focused on the right market and geographical area in order to achieve our vision?

• Are we focusing on the right customers?

Once these questions have been answered, it becomes possible to find ways to deal with the hindrances and hurdles that have been identified.

It is then important to review the roles and responsibilities of each member of the management team to see that all these new responsibilities are included in their job descriptions, and the results that are required are clearly defined in order to meet that business vision.

COMMUNICATING CLEARLY AND SHARING INFORMATION

Change is a constant for small businesses, and keeping your team onside means keeping them informed. Giving lip-service to teamwork isn't enough. According to David Anderson, "I think you get far better results by keeping your people informed of what's going on, making them part of the loop, part of the process. I'm of the view that people are far more capable of making decisions and delivering results if they feel that they are able to do that and you are keeping them informed of the things they need to make the right decisions."

He acknowledges, "My approach is precisely the opposite of those companies that restrict information to the upper levels and do not let it filter down. I think that devalues your employees. I even let financial information go throughout the company. I don't think it hurts the employees to know how well we're doing."

Whether you call it communication, rapport, or feedback, it is a vital part of the human resources aspect of leadership. And it's a two-way street. Being responsive to what your employees tell you creates an atmosphere they'll want to work in.

Both Susan Niczowski (Summer Fresh Salads Inc.) and Mabel Jakimtschuk (Sherwood Village Spa) believe in sharing information and getting feedback from their employees. Susan says, "My management style is listening to people, looking at the pros and cons, and trying to make a decision based on a group decision. Then I'll finalize it or not."

"I share all the decisions that I make with my staff," Mabel says. "I share with them what strategies we should take for the success for the business, how we should treat different clientele and I give them options on products we should focus on. I have a vision that I share this vision with them and then they give me feedback. I listen, analyze and take into consideration the feedback that they give me, and base my decisions on that. It's based on very strong teamwork."

DELEGATING EFFECTIVELY

Entrepreneurs need to share information, and they need to share tasks. A Royal Trust poll of 400 entrepreneurs in the top 10 per cent of self-employed earners found they work an average of 61 hours a week. Many stated that a "willingness to work more hours than most people" was a very important factor in their success.[3] But it is more than just hard work.

Delegating becomes more important as a business grows. Unfortunately, given the independence and self-reliance of the entrepreneurial spirit that drives an individual to start and run a business, delegation often doesn't come naturally to the entrepreneur.

Taking the steps outlined in this chapter to set a clear direction for company growth should involve the small business operator identifying his or her own changing role and the need to transfer certain tasks to others.

In the course of working through many business reorganizations, I have developed a checklist of questions which charts the process of delegation step by step.

DELEGATION STEP BY STEP

Step 1: Preparation

Analyze the job or the tasks that need to be done
Decide what to delegate

Step 2: Plan the Delegation

Key results expected
Time lines
Standards
Budget
Critical interfaces

Step 3: Select the Right Person

Does the work belong to a particular position?
Who has the interest and/or ability?
Who will find the work challenging?
Who will the assignment stretch and help to grow?
Who has been overlooked when you have delegated in the past?
Who has the time?
Who is being prepared for a new assignment or promotion?

Step 4: Communicate the Delegation

Describe fully the project or task and the expected results
Agree on standards of performance and timing
Determine any development or help needed
Define parameters and resources available
Agree on amount and frequency of feedback
Spell out the authority being delegated
Tell others who is in charge

Step 5: Get Feedback as Agreed

Follow-Through
Provide support, resources, information

BUILDING AN EFFECTIVE TEAM: HIRING AND FIRING

The Royal Bank booklet for small business, *Your Business Matters: Starting Out Right*, says, "A team of enthusiastic, motivated employees, dedicated to their careers and your enterprise, is the most valuable resource your company can have."[4] Building the right team, staffed with the right people, requires careful planning and step-by-step implementation. It means:

- Hiring the Right People for the Right Job
- Developing Team Spirit
- Knowing When to Get Rid of a Bad Apple

Hiring the Right People for the Right Job

Putting the right person in the right job can make or break your team. Says Susan Niczowski of Summer Fresh Salads Inc.: "You're only as good as your people, so try to treat people the way we want to be treated. Everyone has good days and bad days, and we scream and we shout, but at the end of the day, we feel that we're part of a family and a team, and that's extremely important." She goes on: "People are extremely important. Sometimes they've got to put in more time than your normal eight-hour shift, but just by treating people with consideration and gaining their respect, they'll put out 150 per cent effort."

Management needs to spend time and energy both to ensure that the company is viewed positively by potential recruits and to make sure it finds quality employees. Hiring the right person with the right skills, knowledge, and attitudes is vital if the business is to succeed.

Developing Team Spirit

Knowing when your team is working and when it is not is important. If things aren't moving forward, then something's wrong.

According to David Haslam, "I try and promote my team leaders to instil confidence and positive attitudes in the employees. You have to motivate in a positive manner. You have to identify what employees have done wrong, but on the other hand, you have to focus on the positive things that they've done right, rather than just yelling at them and telling them what they've done wrong. And I think that makes a world of difference."

He continues, "I like to think I've been successful because I have a good rapport with my employees. Even with my team leaders, my foremen, I implemented a team leader management system and found that part of that system failed. I think my problem was that I had too many team leaders and they were losing focus. So I regrouped my team leadership system and cut it down to size. Now I have just one foreman. He has the right attitude and can direct the men as he sees fit. So he now has even a better rapport than I did."

Building team spirit requires considerable effort. A solid and effective team needs to have a clear vision and goals to achieve, and it also needs:

• capable people who are committed to achieving the goals

• development plans for individuals and opportunities for growth

• feedback on how far we've come in achieving the goals that we've set for ourselves; there's nothing as important as communicating how successful we've all been.

• opportunities to share ideas and views

It's also important not just to focus on the task aspects of the team but also to make sure that people get to know each other well and understand where each of them is coming from. Thus, opportunities for socializing and team building are important so that members of the team can get to know each other. This might be as simple as going out for a beer together one night each week or month.

An effective leader will help team members develop their skills and then be willing to give them the ball and let them run with it. Mabel Jakimtschuk of the Sherwood Village Spa has eight employees who provide clients with a holistic approach to skin-care and body care. "I give them the opportunity to make their own decisions," Mabel explains. "That to me is the reason why the business is successful."

Knowing When to Get Rid of a Bad Apple

When asked to name their biggest management weakness, a sur-prising number of entrepreneurs on The 1998 PROFIT 100 survey of Canada's fastest-growing companies said they were too soft on people. Many said their biggest mistake was not pulling the plug on bad performers or bad attitudes soon enough. And yet putting off the inevitable can be a deadly mistake in a small, growing company built on teamwork and attitude. Failure to eliminate one bad apple will not only permit the rot to continue, it actively encourages further decay; morale among other team members declines as they perceive management's inability to deal with the problem.[5]

For David Haslam, it is essential that the right people be part of his operation. "For me, it's personality and attitude. It has to come from the top and it has to go right to the bottom, no matter who you are. I find that if I have bad apples in my workforce, I weed them out. I explain to them that we really can't have that type of attitude in our organization. It reflects poorly with our clients and with our other employees, and it creates a bad atmosphere."

Chapter 16, "Termination Procedures," will give further advice on how and when to do this. There will be times when an employee simply does not work out. In such cases it is best to end the com-pany's relationship with a problem employee.

ATTRACTING
AND RETAINING
THE RIGHT PEOPLE

It is easy to think of attraction and retention only in terms of compensating people, but as we shall discover, that is only part of the picture. In the present economy, two factors often make it difficult for small businesses to attract and retain the right employees. The first is the scarcity of workers in many fields; despite Canada's steadily high unemployment rate, there is full employment and even a shortage in many of the business areas occupied by small, new companies. The second and closely related factor is the fierce competition that exists for highly educated, skilled, or trained people in areas such as software development, Web-based technologies, biotechnology, and other advanced technological services.

Today a small firm is likely to experience difficulty in hiring the best people, whether it is high tech or low tech, a service provider or a manufacturer. This same problem faces small and growing firms in areas as diverse as trucking, food creation and processing, and software. Failure to attract and keep the needed staff obviously can be a check to growth or lead to even worse

consequences. This is a constant challenge faced by even relatively established and successful smaller firms, such as those on
The 1998 PROFIT 100 list.

So, if you are having this problem, you are not alone. And as
you might expect, business leaders and experts have taken note of
the situation and have revealed ways to deal with it. Effective
methods do exist, but you have to learn them, and then use creativity and flexibility to apply them to your own business situation.

COMPENSATION IS ONLY PART OF THE STORY

Compensation must be reasonably competitive to attract and
retain the best employees in the field, but for a small company,
that is only part of the story. Often, it must combine its compensation offer with other incentives such as: a stimulating,
team-oriented, and flexible work environment; a personal and
responsive atmosphere; opportunities for self-direction, initiative,
reward, and advancement; and creative bonuses including profit
sharing. Large companies can rarely offer these things to the
same degree, although they can usually carry the day in salaries,
benefits, and glitzy facilities.

Compensation, like various other factors, is equally important
in attracting workers and in retaining them. For a small business,
then, the use of compensation in attracting employees must be
coordinated with a complete picture of the company, its culture,
benefits, attractions, and advantages: its "intangibles." Often, in a
small company, compensation will mean having to "compensate,"
for it will be, at best, on a par with large companies in this area.

Compensation is equally important in attracting workers and
in retaining them, as are other factors, such as the small business's natural advantages of creativity, flexibility, scope for initiative, and a feeling of belonging. These intangibles cannot be
offered to a prospective employee unless they have actually been
developed in the corporate culture. And as long as they are oper-
ative in the company, they will be effective not only in attracting
but in retaining and developing the employees.

BASICS OF ATTRACTION AND RETENTION FOR SMALL BUSINESSES

The areas that have a major impact on attraction and retention are:

• Marketing Membership in the Company

• Values-Based Business Goals and Practices

• Flexibility and Good Communications

• Interesting Work and Opportunities for Development

Under all these headings, a small business has potential advantages due to its ability to adapt and shape itself such that it can offer enticing intangibles to prospective employees. But these advantages remain only potential ones until the owners/managers actually and effectively plan them into the company. A small business cannot count simply on the fact that it is small to attract workers looking for something less rigid and more responsive than what larger corporations usually offer.

Marketing Membership in the Company

"Marketing membership," in the modern HR field, means presenting your company as an organization that the best workers will want to belong to. It means structuring and presenting your company as something to which the employee can make an important, creative contribution and be rewarded not only materially but by being integrated into the company as a respected member, not merely a "hire." Most of us are familiar with the ways in which various entities market the advantages of "being on the inside," of being a member: American Express is a prime example. The method is used effectively by a whole range of organizations, from investment dealers to country clubs.

Organizations have to market membership as much as they market products and services, and perhaps more so, because it is just as important to attract the right employees as to attract customers and clients. Growing businesses need to "attract people, hold people, recognize and reward people, motivate people, and serve and satisfy people," writes Rick Spence, in his book *Secrets of Success from Canada's Fastest-Growing Companies*.[1]

It's interesting to place the hiring and retention of good employees under the concept of "marketing." It highlights how important good people are to a business's success and how necessary it is to compete for them. That means having a good product to offer, getting the word out effectively, and then delivering for the "customer" you've attracted. Small businesses potentially possess strong advantages in several crucial areas that are important to many career-seekers. These are basically the areas mentioned above, and they can be effectively marketed to job candidates:

- flexibility and good communications: a flexible work environment, broader-based decision making than in large companies, real dialogue between workers and management

- interesting work and opportunities for development: self-directed, responsible work, including opportunities to take initiative, innovate, and participate in decision making, and to acquire new skills, keep up-to-date in one's specialization, and advance

- innovative forms of bonuses, including profit-sharing (due to its technical nature, this point is fully discussed in Chapter 9, "Incentives")

- the feeling of membership or belonging that the above factors can deliver

The way in which your firm implements such factors will be unique. You need to be aware of marketing these unique qualities to the employment candidates you want to attract.

What Does the Employee Value?

A major advantage of small businesses is their frequent ability to offer forms of work that dovetail with the growing emphasis many people today place on values. There are two ways in which this occurs. First, the business may offer flexibility and a working environment that allows room in the employee's life for what he or she values. Second, the business may offer work and working methods through which the employee can express his or her social values and beliefs on the job.

Drawing on her experience of high growth firms, Lynda Bowles of Deloitte and Touche says, "I think the workforce is changing along with people's needs. Employees no longer live to work. They work to live. Generally they look at a job as providing income, and they are actually willing to take less income to have a more balanced life. They value their leisure time much more than my generation. I know there are people at the office who will simply refuse to work say, Monday nights, because they're got a commitment. And I think you have to respect that."

Lynda went on to say that, "it's important that companies understand the needs of their employees and then try to create an environment to meet those needs. And money isn't always the answer. Sometimes it's more important to have weekends off than to make $10,000 more. What are you going to do with the $10,000 if you don't have time to enjoy it."

The Family-Friendly Workplace

Small businesses can turn to their advantage the growing renewal of "family values." These include all the issues that were once associated with "women in the workplace" but are more and more coming to include men and the entire family. People increasingly look for companies and positions that accommodate things like pregnancies, child rearing, and family togetherness time, and facilitate family life rather than interfere with it. Small businesses have the flexibility to adapt to these demands and benefit from the process.

Lynda Bowles told me of women managers from smaller entrepreneurial companies who had given her examples of flexibility now offered in the workplace. In some cases, children came to the office after school, and if the parent was not there at that time, someone in the office would look after the child. In other cases, when a child was sick, the firm allowed the parent to bring the child to work to provide a support system, or allowed the employee to work from home.

Lynda mentioned that in her own large firm, a regional office was able to institute a weekend day care so that parents working weekends "could bring their children to work. This gave the other spouses at home a break. The children have fun with their friends, and the spouse that's working gets to have lunch and spend time with their children."

Creating this kind of family atmosphere can be very attractive to many prospective employees. For existing employees, good communications on such subjects, leading to flexible management to accommodate their needs, can be a strong motivation to stay with the firm and give it strong commitment.

Work Aligned with Values

The increased desire for leisure time is only the first aspect of changing values and expectations in the workforce. Equally important is the growing demand for meaningful work and a working environment in which the worker can feel respected as a creative contributor not just a functionary. The factors that may work for your company in this respect are many: a socially useful and responsible business goal, a workplace that de-emphasizes subordination and promotes respect, a relative informality that suits the lifestyle and attitude of many younger workers, and other things. These can be significant attractions.

Such things can be significant attractions especially in low-skilled positions in fields such as retail, food services, and housekeeping. The employers of retail clerks or fast-food counter servers frequently have very little room to raise pay. Positions such as these can often be made attractive through flexible management that allows for consultation with the workers leading to variation of responsibilities and work schedules, and the creation of a cooperative and "fun" atmosphere.

Flexibility and Good Communications

Basically, flexibility means giving employees the latitude to set their hours, work at home on occasion, determine the deadlines and other "timeliness" characteristics (i.e., the schedule for preliminary stages that must be established in order to meet a major deadline) of projects they are responsible for, and the like. Such flexibility can be offered in some degree to nearly all employees; it is especially important for creative, self-motivated ones.

To offer this significant advantage to employees and prospects, the company must develop a culture to ensure that flexibility exists and is valued. Management needs to bend when it can to accommodate employees' wishes for flex time, self-chosen holidays, summer work hours, and other such things. It needs to be alert and proactive in recognizing and responding to such desires among employees. It needs to listen and communicate.

For owners this means remembering that the employee has a "real" life and that they must be realistic in expectations and performance assessment/measurement. But this cannot be a casual behaviour that owners or managers exhibit when the mood strikes; it must be an established, clearly communicated, consistently practised feature of the company's values and culture.

Managing Flexibility

Of course, owners and managers must not be allowed to make unrealistic time demands. Good communications and involving employees in decision making can assure that employees are committed to the necessary elements of structure and strictness in their jobs. Managers need to recognize that one employee's flex time may be another's inconvenience in discovering that a co-worker is not around for consultation when needed. Such potential conflicts need to be creatively and diplomatically solved.

Managers must also temper overwork. In a PROFIT article, one company told of a creative employee so highly motivated by its flexible work environment that an ambulance had to take the person to the hospital every six months! As this story indicates, flexibility is likely to give you back in enthusiastic involvement much more productivity than you fear you may lose from lack of structure.

In an article in *The Globe and Mail's* Report on Business, Tom Daniel, vice-president of client and professional services at Necho Systems Corp., Mississauga, Ontario, said, "You have nothing if you don't have fun." Small companies almost always have an advantage in this area, whether it is providing a convivial work environment or enjoyable company outings, such as the half-day employee appreciation event, with "water pistol fights, horseback riding, and wheelbarrow races."

Lynda Bowles effectively summarized the whole subject of flexibility for small businesses. "The large corporations want to be flexible," she said, "but their nature makes it more difficult." On the other hand, she commented, as the owner/manager of a small business you "can adapt your way of doing business to your employees, rather than having the employees adapt."

Interesting Work and Opportunities for Development

Because the best workers have so many options, management's job today "is not to command. It is to inspire," says Rick Spence.[2] PROFIT 100 leaders agree that the future of their organizations hinges on their ability to provide a stimulating and rewarding environment for their staff.

David Haslam of Presidential Plumbing Ltd. in Etobicoke, Ontario, puts his chief principle this way: "I think it's attitude. I want to make sure I have a positive attitude here. I'm always trying to talk about the future and how we're a team, and I like to create an atmosphere where everyone's part of the organization." David links the idea of providing a future, the interesting opportunities for job growth and advancement and improved remuneration, to the idea of a "team" and "family" atmosphere in the workplace. He knows that these go hand in hand and are both vital to retaining good employees long-term. "I try and create an atmosphere where they're comfortable and they really don't want to go anywhere else."

Thus, for many modern businesses, and not just in high-tech areas, it is vital to provide work that is interesting and constantly challenges an employee's creativity, skill, and training. This is linked to the communication factor that can be positively developed especially in small companies. Highly educated individuals know that their own survival depends on state-of-the-art knowledge and skills, and that they cannot maintain these in their "spare time." If the job does not provide constant education and creative advancement, they will leave for one that does. Ownership and management will not know about these aspirations and adapt to meet them if it does not listen and communicate effectively.

Training and career development are among the many issues that show the interdependence of HR planning both to attract and to retain the right people. You might think of these two as the short-term and the long-term aspects of your human resources function.

Opportunities to Grow

"The goal of the company should be to train people out of their position." That was one conclusion reached by participants in The Wisdom Exchange: Accelerating Growth Through Innovation, a 1998 forum of business leaders and experts organized and co-sponsored by the Ontario Ministry of Economic Development, Trade and Tourism and 20 Canadian corporations.

The employee must be offered the opportunity and room to grow and should receive the encouragement, support, and training to take advantage. In the phrase "opportunity and room to grow" the meaning of opportunity is clear. Room to grow means that there is somewhere in the company for the employee to grow to. If you cannot take advantage of your employee's new skills and initiative, then indeed you are training him or her to walk out the door. If you can take advantage of an employee's self-development, then training becomes not just something you do in a mad scramble to keep your people, but something that adds value to your company, because you have planned for and are ready to use it to your profit. A question to ask here, as the Wisdom Exchange participants agreed, is:

How does the individual grow in the company beyond just doing a job?

If you can answer this question, in collaboration with the employee, and in a way that benefits both the employee and your company, then you are well on the way to retaining long-term the employees you hire.

Interesting Work Depends on Good Communications

Strong personal relationships are needed between the owner/manager and the staff, or, in somewhat larger firms, between upper management and staff. But either the small business's operator, or a supervisor directly in communication with the operator, must develop an understanding of employee needs and monitor for opportunities to address those needs.

> As David Haslam said, such ideas cannot merely be "management techniques" but must permeate the whole company, starting with the operator. In the case of Presidential Plumbing Ltd., everything starts with his own attitude: "It's personality and attitude. It has to come from the top, and it has to go right to the bottom, no matter who you are.
>
> "I make it quite clear to my staff and my foreman that even though you have to maintain production and you still have to motivate the employees to work, you have to do it in a positive manner. There's no point in yelling at them and telling them what they've done wrong. You do have to identify what they've done wrong, but on the other hand, you have to focus on the positive things that they've done correctly. And I think that makes a world of difference."

The owner and/or supervisor(s) must not only be personally responsive, they must develop, together with the employees themselves, structured methods to make sure that employee needs are monitored. Performance in this area needs to be consistent, and response needs to be quick. The Wisdom Exchange participants put the above point as follows: "Have a game plan to retain good employees; do not wait for trouble to start."

Kieran O'Briain, president of Kee Transport, tells a story that shows how much his firm depends upon a structured method of monitoring and responding to employee needs. But the story also illustrates how no method can work all by itself: the owner and manager must be alert.

One day, a driver working for Kee called from the road to tell the firm's Edmonton office that he was quitting, and this information was relayed to O'Briain. The driver was on his way to Montreal, so O'Briain had the Montreal manager take him to dinner and investigate the man's dissatisfaction. He complained that he felt "nobody cared" and related that when he was in the Toronto office nobody wanted to talk to him.

"I was there all that day," O'Briain said in frustration, "and my door is always open, but the man claimed he didn't even know I existed. And this is despite the fact that he went through our orientation in Winnipeg. So where was the breakdown? Apparently it boils down to a training issue."

O'Briain also learned from the Montreal manager that the driver's next destination was Winnipeg. So O'Briain contacted the Winnipeg office. "Tomorrow morning, our Winnipeg manager will meet him and ask, 'What did you miss? What did you not understand?' So that even though he may still quit, ultimately we'll at least learn something from it."

As this shows, Kee Transport values communications. Its regional office staff know that one of their major responsibilities is to communicate with drivers. Kee provides training programs to integrate drivers into the company; the owner is fully committed to participating in the whole process. Once a small business reaches a certain size, the whole process must be constantly monitored and adjusted.

TWELVE STEPS TO ATTRACTING AND RETAINING GOOD EMPLOYEES

Strong motivators in attracting and retaining good employees are: being part of the creative process and feeling membership in your company. Those who are just there for the bucks can be easily enticed away to another firm. Anyone can sign a bonus cheque! But the way in which work gets done in your company can draw the people you need to you and keep them with you.

We have already begun to enumerate some of the methods by which you can attract, stimulate, and hold valued company members. What can you offer to job prospects and what can you do in order to hold and stimulate valued company members? My own experience and research, my recent interviews with small business owners and experts, and the testimony of such sources as the Wisdom Exchange, leads to a few major points.

Below is a 12-point overview of the most effective principles now being used by leading human resources experts and practitioners. These points add detail to what has already been said and lay the groundwork for future chapters, where the basic ideas will frequently be returned to and expanded.

1. Hire for attitude and aptitude, train for role and function. The main question with most job openings is whether to fill internally or hire externally. The result of going outside can dramatically affect the morale of existing staff who thought they were ready for a step up. If you take care to hire people with potential for growth and then provide the means and avenues for it, you are more likely to retain highly skilled and motivated employees.

2. Be a leader rather than just the boss. Make your employees a part of the company, the community, or the project. Use techniques such as giving regular updates on the status of the company, its ups and downs, its vision and objectives. This type of forum gives staff members a sense of their importance, breeds loyalty, and is an opportunity to share thoughts and participate in decision making.

3. Poor fit with the company culture is the main reason that new hires do not work out. This re-emphasizes the need to set out clear corporate goals and have hiring procedures that are carefully coordinated with the overall business plan.

4. Prove that employees are the important asset that management likes to claim they are. Corporate culture plays a major role in **PROFIT** 100 companies' attempts to retain and motivate employees. Flat hierarchies, fast decision making, improved communications and employee empowerment are all part of the picture. Remember that to retain good employees, they must continue to buy into the company's culture even if that changes as the company grows. So communications and cooperative decision making are a must.

5. Use work projects and teams. Encourage an open discussion on products, services, and work projects. Work projects and the creation of project teams allow you to group compatible creative people together, provide an atmosphere of belonging and a sense of accomplishment, and identify and reward achievement. Create excitement for new employees with different styles of work such as: self-managed teams, multitask assignments, unstructured work, projects and work groups that match high achievers together. In technical groups, leave time for review of project progress and discussion on any aspect of the process.

6. Create communication. Don't expect to put employees in cubicles and get the job done. Constant communications is a basic in retaining employees.

7. Look for ways of giving the creative employee new responsibilities. Analyze the work done by senior staff and give some of it to that employee. Positive responses can occur when an employee sees that he or she is now doing part of the work formerly done by an owner, executive, supervisor, or foreperson.

8. Send employees on management training courses. The benefit will be twofold: they will be better prepared to assume more responsibility, and they will understand some of the situations that ownership and management must deal with.

9. Provide training. Cross-training for multiple roles within the company can provide richer job satisfaction through variety and opportunity for advancement. Designation/certification-related training can be of particular value to some employees.

10. High-achieving and creative people work better when they are happy and this can be accomplished by fulfilling their need for recognition and appreciation. Recognition awards for superior performance should be established beyond compensation. Timely recognition of contributions and input is important to reinforce the sense of importance and personal contribution to company successes.

11. Provide creature comforts, shared responsibility in the workplace, and fun.

12. Live up to expectations created of jobs for new employees or risk disappointment and early departure. Don't fail to meet the commitments you announced in attracting the employees, especially commitments for training.

This twelfth and final point is another way of re-emphasizing a constant refrain of this book: To retain employees and grow, you must plan into your corporate culture and organization (that is, you must actually possess and deliver) what you offer in order to attract the people you need. This basic coordination of human resources with corporate vision, structure, and management is always key.

PART TWO

THE RECRUITMENT
PROCESS

If we can't manage the human resource piece, we won't have any business. We will not be successful in winning business against stiff competition, and people will not want to work for us if we don't win the bids.

—David Anderson, CANATOM NPM

Is it really as simple as that? If you don't have the right people, you don't get the jobs, and your business folds? Many of the business experts and the entrepreneurs I have worked with over the years would say that it is, indeed, just that simple.

In the five chapters of this part, we will take apart that "simple" formula and identify the components of successful recruiting. We start in Chapter 3 with "Creating an HR Plan," a blueprint for making every hiring decision an integral part of company development. The next four chapters give the procedures for defining the functions and people a company needs, locating good candidates, evaluating qualifications, interviewing applicants, checking references, and writing job offer letters.

CREATING
AN HR PLAN

Whether you have to fire someone who isn't working out, pay the costs of someone who quits, or suffer losses from keeping a person on who is only performing marginally, your business suffers when recruiting isn't done right. The costs of hiring the wrong person are extremely high to any business and particularly for small business. The cost of rehiring and retraining puts both a significant financial and time commitment on the organization. It is estimated that, if you add it all up—including lost productivity and recruiting and retraining costs—the actual cost can be from 30 to 50 per cent of a person's wages and salaries. That is significant, and some entrepreneurs put the cost even higher. For David Anderson, CANATOM NPM's business depends entirely on having the right person for the job. He sees it as a Catch 22 stituation because without good employees you won't win the business and without the business, good people will not want to work for you.

> I t's a question of customer relations, says David Haslam of Presidential Plumbing Ltd.: "The customers don't remember what you do right, but they always remember what you did wrong. You have a five-year history with a client, and you've done millions of dollars worth of work with them. All of a sudden, a bad apple that you've hired, created a few problems and it's going to strain the relationship with the company for quite a while."

Kieran O'Briain of Kee Transport would rather pass up a job than send out an employee who doesn't meet company standards. In the long term, he says, you're hurting your reputation if you do otherwise. "A customer may call up and say, 'We need a driver,' and I don't have anybody who is qualified for the job. They may insist I send whoever I have got, but I won't do it. I'm not going to tarnish my name by throwing some second-rate truck driver out there."

With so much at stake, good recruiting is clearly as fundamental for the small business as it is for the big corporation. And yet the cornerstone of successful recruiting—having a human resources strategy—is too often neglected by the small business operator.

WHERE ENTREPRENEURS GO WRONG IN RECRUITING

A recent issue of **PROFIT**[1] identified five common errors made by entrepreneurs when hiring:

- failing to define the job being offered
- overlooking the importance of corporate culture
- taking sole responsibility for hiring
- failing to prepare for the interview
- providing an inappropriate setting for the interview

The lesson that can be drawn from all of these errors is the need for a plan, an overall strategy that extends from identifying the need to hire a new person to ensuring that the interview is conducted properly. Unfortunately, all too often it's the plan that gets passed over in the rush to keep up with the pressures of a small business. "Creating a strategic plan for a fast-growing oper-ation might seem daunting, but it can be an essential component in developing a proper overall strategy. For example, say you plan to expand into new markets next year. Do you need new people? Should your recruiting begin now so you're ready for the start of next year? How will this planned growth affect your hiring and employee training in the coming months? In many businesses, that type of forward thinking can be rare and too often many human resource issues are resolved on the fly."[2]

CREATING THE HR PLAN

The discussion that follows outlines the steps in creating a human resources plan for recruitment. They are:

1. **Management Identifies Areas for Change.** Management con-ducts regular reviews of operations and identifies areas in which positions and/or employees need to change.

2. **People Management for Change.** Management consults with human resources experts (either in-house or external) to match the company's changing needs with potential solutions: training, shifting personnel, and/or recruiting new employees.

3. **Who Should Be Involved in Recruitment?** Management follows a plan of recruitment which incorporates the best human resources theory and practice available to ensure successful hiring.

   Such a plan can help entrepreneurs avoid the five errors PROFIT identified above. We will now focus on the general struc-ture of the plan and relate it to avoidance of the first three errors: failing to define the job; overlooking the importance of corporate culture; and taking sole responsibility for hiring. (In Chapter 6, "The Interview," we will return to this list for points four and five: failing to prepare for the interview and providing an inappropriate setting for the interview.)

1. Management Identifies Areas for Change

Entrepreneurs should regularly conduct company-wide business reviews, as we noted in Chapter 1. Such an assessment compares current conditions and future goals in a way that naturally raises questions about both jobs and employee performance.

> Karen Flavelle's experience at Purdy's Chocolates provides an excellent example of management identifying the HR implications of a change in operations. "On the factory side things really started to come to a head. Things that needed to happen weren't happening because our plant superintendant quit to pursue his own goals. I was left in charge of the plant and that's not my strength. My strength is marketing. We brought in an HR/LR [Human Resources/Labour Relations] consultant who was a huge help in advising us. If something came up, then I could run it by the consultant and ask her advice."

The management-led review should incorporate ideas from as many sources as possible, from inside the company and from outside sources such as customers, vendors, and regular advisers. The frequency of these reviews varies from once a year to three or four times in a year. Questions asked should include:

- What are the company's goals and objectives?
- Do these goals call for expansion into new markets?
- Are new product lines planned?
- Are changes in technology necessary to stay competitive?
- Will new skills and/or training be required to meet the company's goals and objectives?

Let us see how a highly entrepreneurial computer services company might answer these five questions. The company had grown rapidly and as a result there was a high degree of confusion in terms of what the company's goals and objectives were. So a series of off-site sessions were held with the entire senior management team. The initial sessions defined the company's goals in the following areas:

- What business was it in?
- What were its revenue projections?
- What markets did it want to work in?
- Who were the customers that it really wanted to serve?

It was important to follow this process since each of the team managers had joined the company at a different stage and didn't have a clear or common view of goals and objectives. They then looked at whether the goals they agreed on called for expansion into new markets. Indeed, their review showed that they should expand into a wider geographical area, and should not just market to larger companies but to small and mid-size companies as well.

When considering new product lines, as a services company they decided they could offer far more training and project management services to their existing clients. In terms of technology that was required to stay competitive, they felt that they had to buy and develop more software applications, understand them, and be able to sell and provide those services to their customers. This was critical because the market they were in was extremely competitive, demanding constant reviews of their customers' needs in order to remain up to date with those needs and demands.

In terms of new skills and training, they recognized a constant requirement to have all staff trained in new product offerings and services, which meant budgeting both the time and the money to do that.

The end result of answering all these questions is to make sure that the company has a clear idea of what its business goals are and the kinds of skills and competencies it really requires. Finally, it will help to determine, in terms of skills, training, and numbers, what kinds of people are needed over the coming period—months or years—to fill their business needs.

Building the good human resources recruiting plan starts with management. The entrepreneur OWNS the hiring process and must be an integral part of it. What HR adds is method and also, perhaps, the insight that good hiring begins with company strategy.

Redecorating the space where interviews are done is pointless if no one is sure what skills are needed for the position being filled. According to PROFIT, "The most common, and most costly, mistakes are made when employers don't have a clear understanding of what the job entails, or the type of person best suited to perform it."[3]

Know the Corporate Culture

The second most common error PROFIT identified was over-looking corporate culture when considering a prospective employee. "'Fit' is an intangible but real concern in the work-place. People frequently leave organizations because of a personality or culture conflict. Ensure that the new hire will fit into the new culture, and will enjoy working in this kind of environment. Hiring someone you like, but who does not fit into the culture, is a big mistake."[4]

Many small business owners stress this same idea of making a good fit. There are many demands for the limited resources and management's time in a small business. Perhaps one of the best allocations of these scarce commodities is to use them to ensure that a new employee is going to thrive in the existing corporate environment, which in a small business is very often closely linked to the personality and work ethic of the founder. Susan Niczowski of Summer Fresh Salads Inc.: "I'm very up and have a lot of energy. I try to hire people who are high energy types and aggressive and that applies from our shippers and receivers in the warehouse right up to our receptionist at the front door."

2. People Management for Change

The previous sections concentrate on determining the business plan, knowing the company culture, trying to think about the skills and competencies required to meet future business plans. Looking at the people aspects means getting into the fundamental questions of determining how many people are required with what skills to fulfil the business needs.

After the fundamental questions have been answered (e.g., what new positions, what new skills, etc.) the company should then be in a fairly clear position to determine how many people they need, where they need new people, where they need contract people, and where they need to hire them from.

As an example, any new company in the small, growing business sector will need to look at the market requirements, production requirements, and sales requirements to see whether they need any new positions. Do they need new people? Can they meet the business requirements with the existing staff? Do they need to hire full-time people, contract workers, or temporary employees?

The next thing they need to look at is what kind of skills they require. Do they need people with specific experience? Or do they need people who have worked in the manufacturing sector, with a particular skill operating a certain type of machinery or computer application?

Then the company needs to ask what kind of work experience is necessary. Can they hire people with no work experience? Do they need people who have worked in a particular geographical or market area, or serviced particular customer needs? These are the things that small business owners and management teams need to ask themselves.

Finally, if they've decided they will need more people, they must then think about when they will need them. Do they need them immediately, in a month, at the end of the year? They should also make sure that hiring is done in a planned way so that if new people require training, there's a handover period so they can get that training.

Does the hiring plan involve any employee turnover or attrition? Not all employees stay, in spite of all best efforts. When thinking about human resources planning, do you need to hire an extra person or temporary employee to make up for any turnover that might occur?

After a business review identifies areas of change, the entrepreneur must look at these areas from a new perspective: people management. Do the plans for change translate into different jobs, more jobs, more employees? Wherever possible, the entrepreneur should look for help in answering these questions to those with expertise in human resources, whether in-house or from outside. Company colleagues, too, should be consulted, especially those who work in the area which is about to change.

Some fundamental questions to be answered include:

• What new positions are opening up?

• What special skills (e.g., computer applications) will be needed?

• What work experience (e.g., in a particular geographical area) will be required?

- When will new staff be needed?

- When should hiring be scheduled to ensure a smooth transition?

- Does the hiring plan also provide for employee turnover and attrition?

The bottom line in answering all these questions is that each new hire must contribute to improved company performance.

3. Who Should Be Involved in Recruitment?

All of the small business operators I interviewed were very involved in hiring; in fact, some of them did all of the human resources work for their firms. For them, and for other entrepreneurs in the same position, PROFIT's third recruiting error—taking sole responsibility for hiring—seems to hit uncomfortably close to home. How does a good people manager hire?

The basic answer is you don't do it alone—even entrepreneurs without any in-house staff or any funds to hire consultants have access to human resources expertise. First and foremost, colleagues in the company should contribute to hiring at every stage, from drafting the job description to setting the terms of employment. There are other sources as well. Colleagues and friends in other firms can give advice about how they define the responsibilities of jobs similar to the one you're thinking of adding. Talk to the network of advisers you rely on in other areas for their insights on how other companies are handling recruitment.

And, of course, there is the material in this book. The next several chapters break down the recruitment process into clearly defined steps for you to follow in several areas: job descriptions, finding candidates, interviewing, reference checks, and job offer letters.

Basic at every point is to develop a process in consultation with your employees and then stick with it. For example, Chapter 4 on job descriptions suggests that a manager should take the time to update a job description even for an existing job before beginning to search for candidates. Why? PROFIT explains, "For instance, the secretary who processes invoices every day may also manage payroll or negotiate supplier contracts."[5] The point is that responsibilities can change and as people grow in jobs, they take on more and more work and are expected to do so. Should they leave the company, a new job description needs to be created to reflect those new responsibilities.

The plan should also provide scope for considering several other questions before hiring begins:

• Will the position be full-time, part-time, or contract?

• Are there candidates in-house or is an external search required?

• Will training be provided, or will candidates be required to have the skills needed for the position?

The plan should also address other areas:

• Who will conduct the interviews?

• What type of preparation should be done before the interview?

• Where and how should the interview be done?

Will the position be full-time, part-time, or contract? The reason for asking this question is that, depending on the type of work, there can be different kinds of people to fill various positions. Full-time people tend to expect the job to last for a long time. Part-time people are usually only required for certain parts of the day or week. For instance, bank tellers may be hired to work weekends only. Or in a small business, people may be required to do packing and shipping at certain times of the week or the month. Contract workers are useful for projects that might be completed within a period of two to six months. This might include scouting out a particular market or creating a new software application.

In considering whether you need people on a full-, part-time, or contract basis, the concern is the type of work, but also the payment structures for these different types of employee. Full-time people are more likely to require benefits, whereas part-time and contract people, depending on how long they work, are less likely to. They have clearly defined work terms and, in the case of contract people, will no longer be employed when the task is completed.

Are there candidates in-house or is an external search required? In determining the human resources requirements for the coming months or years, it is important before going out to do an external search, to look to see if there are any people currently employed in the organization who might be suitable for these newly created positions.

Will training be provided, or will candidates be required to have the skills needed for the position? The answer to this question requires that the company determine the likelihood of being able to hire people with the kinds of skills they require or will they have to provide training. Training is often required in cases where it's very difficult to find a certain particularly scarce skill, or where there's a shortage of qualified people. As we found in the sample of entrepreneurs interviewed, companies prefer to hire people who've already got the skills and thus avoid the cost of training.

The company should consider, however, that in particularly tight labour markets, such as in the high-tech sector, the provision of training may be one way of attracting people to join the company, as this differentiates them from many other organizations. However, the company has to look at the costs of such training and whether they will get a return on investment for that training.

Who will conduct the interviews? Typically, it should be the person to whom the new employee would report. This would be the key person to conduct the interviews, but since it's important that an individual fits into the culture and environment of the company, it's sometimes helpful to have the owner of the company interview the person as well. Some of the colleagues who will be working with the person should also be involved, because fit, as we discuss in this book, is vital to employee retention.

What type of preparation should be done before the interview? Before the interviews take place, all of the people doing them should first review the candidate's résumé to understand the background of the person who is going to be interviewed. It is also necessary to understand the requirements for the position. That is why it's important that the person doing the interviewing has read the job description and competency pro-file for the position so they can answer any questions from the candidates.

Third, it's important to understand the environment in which the individual will work—the department or the area—to be able to see if that individual will fit. Finally, it's essential to prepare appropriate questions to ask the individual. We cover this later in Chapter 6, "The Interview."

Where and how should the interview be done? The inter-view should ideally be done in the workplace. However, this isn't always practical as there may not be a room suitable for con-ducting an interview. In this case it's advisable to get a hotel room or a room in some organization like the Board of Trade in which to conduct the interview.

In some cases, if the candidate works a considerable distance from the organization, it may be necessary to do the interview over the telephone, or if possible, at a conference core site. It is usually helpful to see a person's face and their reactions to ques-tions during the course of the interview.

Job descriptions and competency profiles are useful for many things besides the hiring process. For instance, they can be used for:

• determining bonuses

• terminations

• promotion and career planning aspects

Bonuses, for example, can be determined on the basis of "expected results." These can be viewed each quarter, half year, or annually, whenever the bonus is paid out, and compared to the results that were achieved. If the results that were achieved were in line with those that were expected, it can be assumed that 100 per cent of the bonus will be paid out. Anything less would necessitate a prorating of the bonus. For instance, if only half the objectives were met, you'd only pay out 50 per cent of the expected bonus.

If none of the results were met, then you would have to decide the next appropriate step, for example, additional train-ing and support. If after further training there was still no improvement, the company would then have to consider termination of the individual.

The entry level requirements and personal competencies outlined in the job description are extremely useful in the hiring process in determining the kind of person you want, both in terms of experience and personal characteristics. For instance, if you need somebody with high energy and you determine in the interview that the candidate is rather low in energy and unable to change, then it would not be a good idea to hire that person for the organization.

In terms of career development, the various specified technical and general competencies can be used as a way to determine prospects for movement within the company. For instance, all job descriptions and competency profiles should note the technical and general competencies for every position in the company.

In the example shown, if the administrative assistant wants to move on to a job in sales administration, it would be helpful to look at the competencies required in that job description to see how they might prepare themselves to take on the job. For instance, under technical competencies, they may have to learn a specific new skill relating to computer software. In the area of general management, they would probably have to be very good at organizing events, making calls to customers, and so on.

CHAPTER FOUR

JOB DESCRIPTIONS AND COMPETENCY PROFILES

Job descriptions seem foreign to the entrepreneurial spirit. In a small business, especially in the crucial start-up phase, doesn't everybody do everything? Isn't the willingness to pitch in and do whatever needs doing one of the things the entrepreneur prizes above all? Formal job descriptions may even seem an unnecessary chore when just keeping the business open is more than a full-time job. But when a company starts growing, especially in numbers of employees, it's important to start drafting job descriptions. Think of job descriptions as a sign that your business is getting somewhere, that you are going through a rite of passage every successful firm must negotiate.

Susan Niczowski of Summer Fresh Salads Inc. has relied on job descriptions throughout the growth of her company to track changes in the duties of existing positions and to define relationships between workers and departments. "When we first started we had one person handling everything in the office and now there are five people. Basically, going from two people to an 86-person operation, you've got various people reporting to various people and their job descriptions would have changed over the years."

Susan's experience tallies with my own observations from years in human resources. Small business operators will manage more effectively if they take the time to create job descriptions and review and update them regularly. In the previous chapter we saw that all work assignments within a company must make sense within the context of its overall strategy. Thus, crafting a job description should begin by determining how the position being defined will contribute to profitability. Once the small business operator has decided that the position is actually needed within the organization, he or she is ready to draft the job description.

DEFINING JOB DESCRIPTIONS

A job description is a brief but detailed document which gives three pieces of information about a position:

1. the duties and responsibilities attached to it

2. performance expectations for someone in the position

3. the skills, qualities and experience—the competencies—needed to function effectively in the position

The first two terms used here are probably familiar to entre-preneurs. "Duties and responsibilites" refer to tasks to be performed by an employee: operate switchboard, make travel arrangements for sales staff, load and unload transport vehicles. "Performance expectations" quantify the volume of work expected: 150 client contacts booked per month, 10 per cent year-over-year increase in sales revenue.

The third term, "competencies," is increasingly used to name the skills and knowledge a person requires to perform a particular job. Thus, a list of competencies for a switchboard operator might include an excellent telephone manner and familiarity with the type of switchboard console a company is using. Characterizing skills and knowledge as competencies is intended to focus on the requisite qualifications rather than specifying the means by which those qualifications were obtained.

A SAMPLE JOB DESCRIPTION
WITH COMPETENCY PROFILE

The following job description and competency profile for an administrative assistant was created for a specific medium-size company but is generic enough to apply to a number of companies. It contains the various points covered in this chapter. The responsibilities and expected results are defined, so that it is clear what results an administrative assistant is expected to achieve. The competencies—the skills, knowledge, and behaviours—required for this position are defined in terms of general, technical, and personal competencies. The description is useful for both recruiting administrative assistants and for creating individual development plans to make up for any gaps that might be missing in terms of skills and knowledge.

Administrative Assistant Job Description and Competency Profile

Overview

An administrative assistant holds an entry-level support position and works under the direct supervision of several senior staff.

Responsibilities

- provide day-to-day administrative support for staff, including handling all faxing, filing, and photocopying requests
- coordinate and set up meetings internally and externally
- coordinate all travel arrangements for group members
- lend administrative support and provide relief to other administrative staff and their areas as required
- provide occasional reception relief
- take messages

Expected Results

- ensure that assigned responsibilities are completed efficiently, effectively, and on time
- demonstrate high standards of service excellence (work to be error free)
- deliver results on time
- work well with internal staff, suppliers, and customers

Entry Level Criteria

- high school diploma or equivalent
- two years' experience in the workforce
- strong, current, and general computer skills including word processing and electronic mail
- excellent interpersonal and telephone skills
- basic knowledge of office administration

Technical Competencies

- strong demonstrated working knowledge of all computer programs used by company
- ability to create presentations using computer programs used by company
- excellent telephone manner
- working knowledge of the main switchboard console

General Competencies

- able to organize and plan support in his/her area
- able to organize and plan company events and to arrange meetings and associated logistics to the company standards

Personal Competencies

• hard worker with high energy and enthusiasm

• team player; assists other group

• meticulous worker, with flawless attention to detail

• responsible worker, with ability to meet deadlines

WRITING A JOB DESCRIPTION

There are three crucial areas of the job description:

• duties and responsibilities

• performance expectations

• competencies

When writing a job description, be detailed and wherever possible quantify expectations (four years' experience as computer programmer, 300 invoices processed weekly). Information should be detailed but not so particular as to overshadow points you wish emphasized or so rigid as to discourage initiative on the part of the person doing the job.

For example, in advertising for a graphic designer, you should give prominence to the software packages currently in use and to the volume of work expected; you should not list by title and length all the projects completed in the previous year. Offering specifics of recent production as a guideline could give innovative workers the impression that you would not be open to improvements in method which could increase productivity.

Duties and Responsibilities of the Job

1. Name the essential responsibilities of the position, if possible.

2. Spell out areas of responsibility clearly in order to avoid clashes over authority. Identify the position within the organizational structure of the company.

3. Spell out any special physical requirements of the position, such as lifting heavy objects or prolonged use of computers.

On point one, that the responsibilities of a job description should be quantified, note that the sample job description above quantifies several of the six responsibilities given. The assistant will do "all" faxing, filing, and photocopying, and make "all" travel arrangements. Reception relief will be an "occasional" responsibility of the assistant.

On point two, that areas of responsibility should be spelled out, the sample job description specifies that the administrative assistant will be working "under the direct supervision of several senior staff." The assistant is expected to provide services on an equal basis for all these senior staffers: giving administrative support, setting up meetings, and coordinating travel arrangements. In addition, the senior staff may direct the assistant to help other members of the company administration as needed. Thus, the job description places the new position clearly within the company structure and provides a rule for resolving potential disputes over the assistant's availability.

On point three, that any special physical requirements should be spelled out, the sample job description does not identify any such requirements for the administrative assistant position. Job descriptions for delivery persons, for example, might emphasize the particular vehicle used for making deliveries—bicycle, automobile, van, etc., along with a range of package size which the delivery person must be capable of lifting without assistance.

Performance Expectations

1. Identify the level of output expected (processing 300 invoices each week).

2. Spell out targets for productivity improvement (increasing sales by a stated percentage per month).

3. Tie performance to quantifiable goals according to a timetable for review (quarterly or annually).

Performance expectations build on the list of duties and responsibilities by quantifying both entry-level production standards and goals for improvement. The sample job description emphasizes at several points that the administrative assistant must prepare documents on time and error-free. It also suggests that the volume of work varies and may be increased by projects passed along from other administrators. It does not, however, give any specific quantities of phone calls to be answered, documents to be faxed and photocopied, or reports to be published.

If you have not quantified a job's output, preparing a new job description is a valuable opportunity to study what volume of work is actually being generated from the position that is to be filled. You may wish to review production over several months in order to develop both a current standard and a target for growth. For example, a sales representative may currently serve 20 accounts within the province of Ontario; planned expansion into Manitoba requires the new sales representative to maintain service for the Ontario clients while adding five new accounts in the new territory.

Such performance expectations will be useful, also, in judging an employee's progress, especially if you maintain a schedule of regular performance reviews in which an employee's work is compared with the results set out in the original job description. Exceeding goals could warrant a bonus or a promotion; it might also suggest a redefinition of the responsibilities of the current job. Failure to meet goals could be the sign that targets were not realistic or that the employee needed guidance or training to reach them. These performance expectations should then be used as a basis for performance evaluations (Chapter 13), and wage and salary reviews (Chapter 8).

Competencies Required for the Position

There are generally three types of competencies: technical, general, and those relating to personal attributes.

Technical Competencies

Technical competencies are the skills and knowledge required for a specific position.

1. Write out the specific technical skills and knowledge required (expertise with a particular computer application; skill with a particular tool; level of previous work experience in the specific industry or market).

2. Highlight any particular qualifications required (a degree in a specific discipline, such as electrical engineering; completion of an apprenticeship; a professional designation, such as chartered accountant; a heavy goods vehicle licence).

3. Specify any particular work experience you consider essential (e.g., shift work).

On point one, the sample job description lists specific technical skills: "strong working knowledge of all computer programs used by company," and "working knowledge of the main switchboard console." The employee must bring to the company this knowledge, not expect training to be provided. The job interview for the position could incorporate brief, representative tests on the equipment used in the job.

On point two, the sample job description lists a specific qualification: "ability to create presentations using computer programs." Candidates might be asked to bring to the interview a sample of a presentation created on the desktop publishing package the company currently uses. The candidate might also be asked to comment on company documents as a way of demonstrating familiarity with the presentation software in use.

On point three, the sample job description indicates that the position requires "two years' experience in the workforce" and characterizes the sorts of office skills that should have been gained from this previous employment: general computer skills such as word processing and electronic mail, office administration, and telephone etiquette.

Technical competencies are very useful in the interviewing process. The interviewer can use them as the basis for testing an applicant's readiness for the job.

General Competencies

General competencies include skills and knowledge that are more generic to a number of jobs or positions, such as skills in communications, innovation, teamwork, time management, and leadership. The best person for a position has such general skills as well as the right technical skills. How often have you brought in a person who possessed the technical skills needed but who failed because he or she was not good in dealing with other people or was disorganized?

1. Write down competencies that are important to this position (skills in customer relations, in working with others, and in written and oral communications).

2. Distinguish between the competencies expected of a person new to the position and of someone who has been in the job long enough to be expected to perform at a fully satisfactory level. This range of expectations will help with training as well as with salary and wage adjustment.

In the sample job description, the general competencies named—"able to organize and plan support" and "able to organize and plan company events and to arrange meetings"—emphasize that the administrative assistant must be capable of organizing and working independently on a large volume of tasks.

No distinction is made, however, between entry-level competencies and the level of skill expected once the employee has gained some experience in the position. Such distinctions are worth making, particularly as guidelines for performance appraisals. For example, the assistant might have been asked to begin with internal meetings, but with the requirement that responsibility for all meetings, both internal and external, would be transferred to the position within six months.

In the same way, you might list among a desktop publisher's general competencies a familiarity with copy editing, but distinguish between a general knowledge at the time of entry and a thorough acquaintance with the special vocabulary and abbreviations of your industry by the end of the first three months.

Personal Competencies

While the distinction is not an absolute one, HR practice speaks of one other type of competency: personal competencies. Here we are trying to acknowledge the importance of certain vital traits that often seem to be the result of inherent personality rather than of training or experience. These are therefore more likely to be gained by hiring people already possessing them than by seeking to develop them through on-the-job programs.

Energy, initiative, integrity, discipline, reliability, adaptability, and willingness to work are all personal competencies. It is notable that these are some of the qualities that the entrepreneurs I interviewed said they considered most important in a successful employee. Personal competencies are vital when seeking a person who will fit in with the culture of the company. For example, if the company is dynamic and fast-paced, you will want to recruit a person who is creative, energetic, and enthusiastic. If the business places heavy emphasis on dealing with customers, then you are looking for reliability and good people skills.

HOW TO PUT THE JOB DESCRIPTION TO WORK

The small business operator can expect to get value from the job description at every crucial point in an employee's work life:

- in the hiring process
- in training and development
- in times of change

The Job Description in the Hiring Process

A well-written job description helps at every stage of hiring, from developing a list of candidates through drafting the job offer letter. The next three chapters will describe recruitment step by step: finding candidates (Chapter 5), interviewing them (Chapter 6), and checking references and writing the letter offering the job to the successful candidate (Chapter 7). The job description has a role to play in each step.

Finding the right person for a job opening is rarely easy. You must take time from regular operations for the unusual tasks of writing and arranging for postings of the job, both internally and outside the company; consulting with your network of industry connections; and inserting advertisements in newspapers and trade publications. A solid job description will make all of these tasks easier, since it will provide the basis for all written notices of the position and also give you specifics to mention when discussing the opening. In particular, when developing a list of candidates to be interviewed, an entrepreneur can use the job description to:

- spread news of the position by providing a clear formulation of duties, expectations, and qualifications
- attract likely candidates because of the clarity of the information given about the opening
- screen candidates—potentially the most onerous step in the process—using it as a checklist of things to look for in résumés

In the interview phase, the job description should be used as the basis for a standardized list of questions put to every candidate. Meaningful comparisons between candidates are possible because of the clear standards set forth in the job description.

Finally, a job description is useful in determining what type and amount of compensation is likely to attract top candidates because it makes meaningful comparisons possible with industry-wide pay scales for similar positions.

David Anderson of CANATOM NPM points out the importance of the job description for maintaining competitive pay scales. "We have a set of job families, job descriptions, and pay scales. We need to have some structure and our pay scales have to be comparable to others both in the market place and in our parent companies. Since a significant percentage of our employees are engineers, we follow very closely what the engineering profession is doing in the provinces that we employ these engineers."

The Job Description in Training and Development

The usefulness of the job description does not end when a new position is filled. The job description should be consulted for guidance on employee training and development and in performance reviews. For example, the sample job description specifies that the new administrative assistant must be familiar with all software used by the company. The entrepreneur may decide that the best candidate is one who knows all the packages except the one used for desktop publishing; the administrative assistant is hired on the understanding that within six months a course on the desktopping program will be completed. The first performance review after six months should verify that the course was taken and that the assistant has begun producing desktopped documents.

Regular updates of job descriptions enable the small business operator to take into account changes in volume of work and in type of work being done at each position of the company. Such a review should be part of a regular business review (as described in Chapter 1) both to identify areas where hiring is necessary and to head off potential conflicts over areas of responsibility.

The Job Description in Times of Change

In a time of change, a job description becomes an invaluable tool for ensuring continuity. For example, when an employee leaves a position, the entrepreneur should consult with him or her about whether or not the description on file still matches the actual work being done in the position and to gain advice about what qualifications are needed for a replacement.

An up-to-date job description is also very helpful in the difficult process of termination, since it provides a way of specifying the shortcomings of performance which lie behind the decision.

The importance of job descriptions in times of change is underscored by Joan Berta of the Canadian Association of Family Enterprises (CAFE) in commenting on the frequency with which succession issues are handled in family businesses without reference to job descriptions, frequently with unfortunate results. Joan told me, "You'll typically find that a lot of the businesses, particularly the smaller ones, don't think about the suitability of the person to the position. The owner's son or daughter automatically comes into the business even if he or she may not have the skills. If there's no job description in place, there's no clear rules. Till their dying day Father or Mother calls the shots, telling everybody what they have to do, and a lot of frustration and animosity can build up with the kids. And as a result, succession is not successful, if it happens at all.

"It's an interesting phenomenon that if we worked for another employer—say IBM or Royal Bank—all the job descriptions would be in place. We'd interview for that position, and we'd pick the most suitable candidate who had the best background and all the qualifications for that job. But we don't think about doing that with our own business".

CHAPTER FIVE

SOURCES OF CANDIDATES

This chapter will look at the various sources that small and medium-size companies use to find potential candidates for their new and existing positions. It will also cover ways of screening applicants.

SOURCES

The top ten sources of candidates for small and medium-size companies are:

1. Referrals by Friends, Business Colleagues, and Employees
2. Personal Contacts
3. Drop-ins
4. Newspapers Ads
5. Creative Advertising
6. Web Sites

7. School Campus Recruiting

8. Industry, Trade, and Professional Associations and Recruiting

9. Headhunters

10. Human Resources Development Canada

1. Referrals by Friends, Business Colleagues, and Employees

These kinds of referrals are among the most highly used forms of recruitment for any firm but are of particular benefit to small and medium-size businesses.

ADVANTAGES AND DISADVANTAGES OF REFERRALS

Advantages	Disadvantages
• It is inexpensive. • People who know your culture are likely to refer candidates who will fit in well. • The reputation of people doing the referring will be enhanced if they recommend good quality people. That is why it is unlikely that they will refer people who are not potentially of good quality. • It is a faster method of getting candidates than going through other sources.	• It may take up unnecessary time since you may feel obligated to interview all the candidates who are referred to you, even if they are not suitable for the position or are not a match for the culture. • Relationships may be destroyed if people continue to refer inappropriate candidates.

How to Ensure Good Referrals

Make sure every employee knows the skills and competencies you're looking for and has a good understanding of the type of person who will fit in with the culture. Reward employees who find new employees. Many companies give substantial dollar amounts to those employees who have referred a hire, providing that individual stays with the company for a specific period of time. This is still inexpensive and is a very effective way of bringing people into the company.

Kieran O'Briain of Kee Transport explains how he rewards his employees who refer new hires. "We have a referral program through our truck drivers. We give the drivers $1,500 for every driver they bring in. It is paid in three instalments. The driver gets $500 if the person is hired, $500 after three months if the person stays, and another $500 if the person stays for six months. We give our drivers business cards, so they can give them to other drivers they meet in coffee shops or truck stops. The numbers of all our offices are on the back of the cards, and they can call any of these. The business card of the person who made the referral is then stapled to the application form."

2. Personal Contacts

Many small and medium-size business owners and managers rely on personal contacts to fill their staffing requirements. They either use personal contacts to fill a position, or they use these contacts as a way of finding people.

David Anderson of CANATOM NPM relies heavily on personal contacts to fill staffing requirements. He does this primarily because he needs to find people who have worked with nuclear technology and finds that the best way to do this is through his network.

He explains, "We'd done an internal resource assessment of what our pool is like, the strengths and the weaknesses. We extended that to our parent companies to see what sort of depth that might fit the operating plant services area and what resources were available there. We came to the conclusion that we didn't have everything we were going to need. Five of us who had previously worked for Ontario Hydro individually compiled a list of all of the names that we could think of, of potential people that we thought could be of help to us.

"We created a single list which we shared and that prompted us to add some more names. We came up with a pool of something like 150 or 160 names on that list, just from our own data bank. We asked our human resources person to contact each one of those to establish if in fact they were interested; if they were available, they were asked for a copy of their résumé.

We then created an electronic database and scanned each individual's résumé into this. The database is available to all of us here. I can pull it up and can see when somebody last spoke to person X, what their current thinking and availability is, and we've just kept in touch with them that way. When we speak to contacts we ask if they know of anybody else that might be interested, and that is how we've developed a network."

He continues, "I would think that personal contact has produced about 80 per cent of the staffing that we've needed, and advertising has produced maybe 20 per cent."

ADVANTAGES AND DISADVANTAGES OF PERSONAL CONTACTS

Advantages	Disadvantages
• It's inexpensive. • You know the people and their work experience. • You know if they will fit with the culture.	• If personal contacts do not work out, there may be a reluctance to let them go. • You may be tempted to "make" them fit a position, because you want to hire them, even though the fit is not there.

3. Drop-Ins

This approach, which simply consists of accepting and screening applications from people who ask about employment due to the visibility or reputation of the company, is widely used by many small and medium-size businesses.

ADVANTAGES AND DISADVANTAGES OF DROP-INS

Advantages	Disadvantages
• It's inexpensive, and people often know the kinds of jobs that the company has. • It provides a constant stream of job applicants.	• As with other methods, you may get résumés from people who are not suitable. They are attracted by your company and come in even if they do not have the skills that are needed.

Karen Flavelle of Purdy's Chocolates notes that she gets a number of people through drop-ins. "In the stores we get a lot of people coming to us because our people look happy in their work. When people are busy they tend to look happier, and in our stores you are always busy. Customers see this and think that this is a nice place to work. So quite a lot of our people in the store come in this way, and they do enjoy it because we have very low turnover."

Mabel Jakimtschuk of Sherwood Village Spa also uses drop-ins as a way to recruit staff. She says: "I hardly ever advertise. It's a small industry and the network is not that large. If people know that you provide a good atmosphere with high-class clientele and high-quality work, they will want to work with you. My reputation is good, so I have people calling all the time asking for work. Before I think about hiring them I consider their personalities."

4. Newspaper Ads

This method of finding candidates is still quite widely used. A Royal Bank survey showed that this form of advertising accounts for up to 50 per cent of all new hires.[1]

Let's take a look at a newspaper advertisement.

DRIVERS WANTED

We have 10 positions for drivers for long hauls
from Brampton, Ont. to Thompson, Ga.
Earning potential of $100,000 per year.
Applicants need to have a commercial licence and
meet DOT requirements.
Please contact us at: the Company Phone Number,
the Fax Number, and the Web site.

This is a good advertisement because it:

• tells you the position, i.e., driver, although it could be more specific as to the type of driver required

• is specific about the number of openings: 10 positions

• gives details about the types of journeys the drivers will have to make, i.e., from Brampton, Ontario, to Thompson, Georgia

- explains earning potential, although it does not say how it is earned, e.g., base salary, overtime, and bonus components
- outlines the specific skills and competencies to fill the position: possessing a commercial licence and the DOT requirements
- tells the reader how to contact the company: by means of a telephone call, fax, or the company's Web site

How Do You Write a Newspaper Ad?

A good newspaper advertisement contains the following points:

- a clear and attractive eye-catching layout
- the minimum number of words to tell the reader exactly what's required and how
- is direct and specific about
  - what the company is
  - what it does (you don't have to mention the company's name, but at least explain what it does)
  - what its location is
  - the job itself (describe in brief detail what the job requires)
- gives details of the type of person required—you can't put in age, but you can say whether you want them to be experienced or mature, and the kind of experience they should have
- is specific about the skills and knowledge required—specific computer skills or a comptroller's designation
- is clear on the methods of contacting the company, whether it be by phone, walk-in application, fax number, or the Web site

Where Do You Actually Place These Advertisements?

There are a number of places to put a job advertisement.

Local paper: These are useful for junior positions and in cases where the company needs local people who don't have to travel very far to work. The advantage of such papers is that they provide a relatively inexpensive form of advertising.

National and Big City Papers: These are useful if you're looking for more senior positions and need to attract people from either an entire city or the whole of Canada, and in some cases, other countries. They are also useful for trying to attract people with a specific expertise, e.g., national sales manager, president, chief financial officer. Other points to note: if you're looking for bilingual candidates who can speak both French and English, it is helpful to advertise in Montreal or any of the other bilingual cities such as Ottawa or Moncton. Also, if you're looking for people who can speak Cantonese or other Chinese languages, it can be useful to advertise in areas that have large Chinese-speaking populations such as Vancouver and Toronto.

ADVANTAGES AND DISADVANTAGES OF NEWSPAPER ADVERTISING

Advantages

- It is effective when the job responsibilities and competencies are well defined.
- It reaches people in the local community if you so target it; this cuts down on relocation costs.

Disadvantages

- It is more expensive than some of the other candidate sources.
- It may bring in many applications that are not a particularly good fit for the position being advertised.

The use of newspaper advertisements may mean a long recruitment process. Since the good candidates you locate via this method may be sending applications to a number of sources, it is important to interview the better applicants as quickly as possible. And it is equally important to make decisive choices as soon as you have interviewed and checked out your candidates. Otherwise the better candidates may be hired away before you act.

5. Creative Advertising

Some companies have become very creative in the ways they use to find candidates. They may still place ads in the newspaper, but they use other innovative methods, as well. Kieran O'Briain of Kee Transport has a different approach to advertising for drivers. "If they don't have business cards, our drivers will give out their pair of gloves with the phone number on them closeup, and they'll get a new pair. They are great gloves."

He also has a motor home that has the company name on it and is furnished as an office so that people can apply for jobs inside. The motor home is also taken to truck stops and large truck shows and conventions.

As well as the examples noted above from Kee Transport, other forms of creative advertisements are:

• Placing advertisements at the checkouts of supermarkets and fast-food restaurants

• Job advertisements placed on the notice boards of community centres, supermarkets, and fast-food restaurants

• Job ads at trade fairs and trade shows—these need to be put in the booths of the various exhibitors

• Posters on lamp-posts on the street, but make sure the posters are large enough for people to see from their cars

• Fliers through doors and you might want to include refrigerator magnets, which are an inexpensive, effective, and eye-catching form of giving out a company's name and job advertisements

ADVANTAGES AND DISADVANTAGES OF CREATIVE ADVERTISING

Advantages

• The method is often eye-catching.
• It can target the type of people and the community you want to hire and is limited only by your ingenuity.

Disadvantages

• It can be expensive, depending on the methods you use.
• Others will copy successful methods, so the advantage may only be maintained for a short period.

6. Web Sites

More and more employers and candidates are using Web sites as part of their recruitment and job-seeking processes. Companies can place job postings on their own Web sites or surf the net to find other recruitment Web sites. For instance, Jobshark and Globecareers.com are clearing houses for job seekers and employers and are quite widely used. When companies set up their own Web sites, potential candidates are able to read the advertisements and send in their applications via computers.

Tips on Setting Up a Good Web Site

You can find someone who is skilled at setting up a Web site either through a referral or by looking in the phone book. Make sure you do reference checks on these firms and get referrals from other companies and follow up on them. Lots of people claim to be Web site designers but may not have the kind of experience or fit that you require. Make sure they are technically able to support you and can redesign and change the site frequently to ensure that it reaches and attracts the kind of people you are after.

Start small. Make sure, in the beginning, that you're able to put job ads up on the site. Once you see how many responses you get from this form of advertising, you can build in a facility so that candidates are able to submit their résumés on-line immediately.

The Web site shouldn't replace traditional methods of advertising but should complement them. Make sure the Web site's address is featured in all your company publications and on business cards so that people know how to reach the Web site and send their résumé to it.

A company I know, recently had a presentation from a Web site designer aimed specifically at the recruitment market. The company was told that the total cost of designing and maintaining the site, which allowed for instant job ad placement and for candidates to submit their résumés, was in the order of $86,000 per year. This was for a medium-size company of about 700 people. Company personnel were surprised to find that the cost of that kind of service by the Web site company for a whole year was the same as putting one full-page advertisement in *The Globe and Mail*. It was immediately concluded, after all the references had been checked, that this was a relatively inexpensive and extremely effective form of reaching job candidates.

When you move to a more sophisticated Web site, try to build in an automated response system that will advise candidates immediately that their résumé has been successfully received. By doing this, you will reduce the number of phone calls to your company asking if résumés have been received.

The final point is to ensure that you are in a position to handle the increased flow of calls. Of course, we're making the assumption that the Web site reaches quite a number of people and that you will be inundated with résumés. If this is the case, make sure you have enough people (contract or full-time) to screen the résumés and select good candidates for you to interview.

Setting up a Web site is very useful these days, particularly since nearly everybody can have Internet access. Even those who don't have home computers now have access through their local library or community centre. This makes it an attractive form of advertising. Once the site is set up, it is also relatively inexpensive compared to other methods, but of course, you'll have to make sure that you get the appropriate quality and number of résumés to justify the expense.

ADVANTAGES AND DISADVANTAGES OF WEB SITES

Advantages

- It is a quick and effective way of matching employers and potential candidates.

- More information can be inexpensively conveyed than by other methods. Companies can effectively illustrate their culture. For instance, they can quite clearly, perhaps even humorously, define the kind of people they want and don't want.

Disadvantages

- Your ad can only be seen by those with computers and Internet access.

- To some degree the method is limited because not everyone is accustomed to looking for positions in this way.

As with some of the other methods, it is necessary when locating candidates through Web sites to have a fast follow-up, because potential candidates will be applying to many other Web sites and job advertisements.

Web sites are a particularly useful way for high-tech companies to search for people since qualified candidates are more likely to have computers and access to Web sites and are equally likely to be familiar with the Internet; in fact, these very qualities may be part of the job description that a company is trying to fill. Managerial, professional, and other positions demanding a lot of education, as well as technical and scientific ones, can be usefully recruited via Web sites.

You will need to have a professional create your Web site and research others in order to be competitive with other firms and organizations that are also looking for candidates this way. Only familiarity with the Web can assure you that your message has the best chance of reaching good candidates, and that you, in turn, are discovering the best Web sites where job-seeking candidates may be posting their qualifications.

7. Campus Recruiting

Going directly to university, college, and high school campuses is a very effective way of recruiting talent with specific skills, particularly for high-tech industries and trade-specific positions.

ADVANTAGES AND DISADVANTAGES
OF CAMPUS RECRUITING

Advantages

- It allows companies to hire specific skills, especially by going to campuses that train for those particular skills.

- It can develop long-term relationships with those schools who can point specific candidates your way.

- It is a source of talent that can be trained in your particular way of doing things and can be moulded to your own culture.

- Career fairs and on-campus recruitment help to build your reputation in the market place as an employer in a particular business, industry, professional, or technical field.

Disadvantages

- The competition is fierce. Companies from all across North America often compete on campuses for the same kinds of skills, particularly in a hot market.

- Presentation and marketing tools have to be very professional since companies must compete against very large organizations that can offer expensive giveaways and other inducements.

8. Industry, Trade, and Professional Associations and Recruiting

Companies looking for particular skills often go to industry, trade, and professional associations that provide job postings and sources of candidates. This is especially relevant to those companies wanting skills in such areas as engineering, accounting, and specific trades.

ADVANTAGES AND DISADVANTAGES OF RECRUITING THROUGH ASSOCIATIONS

Advantages

- You can target a market with specific skills.

- This is an inexpensive source of recruits. Some associations offer fairly cost-effective ways to provide candidates to you.

- You often know the companies that the candidates are applying from.

Disadvantages

- You may be swamped with résumés.

- Often there is no filtering of application forms, so the quality of résumés or applications may not be consistent.

9. Headhunters

Recruitment firms are particularly useful for finding senior staff. It is important to determine up front an appropriate way of working with these companies and coming to an agreed-upon contract. For instance, you may want to make arrangements for the recruitment firm to refund some or all of its fees, or find another person for you, should a candidate not work out within a given period of time.

Headhunters, or recruitment firms, are a huge and growing source of new hires, particularly in the high-tech field and for senior employees. Typically, a recruiting firm will charge anywhere from 20 to 40 per cent of the salary and bonus costs of a new hire's annual earnings. Therefore they are only used for senior positions and those that are difficult to fill. How do you find them?

- Word of mouth

- Look them up in the telephone directory

- Ask local Chambers of Commerce or professional and trade associations you belong to

It's certainly important to interview a number of firms to make sure that they are familiar with the kind of positions you want to fill, that they have experience dealing with your field, and that you feel comfortable with the particular recruiter.

Headhunters may charge only when they find a suitable candidate or they may charge on a project by project basis. The advantage of going on a project basis is they don't just throw any candidate at you in the hope of making money. So my advice would be to contract on a project basis and pay only at the end of the project, when they have found a suitable candidate for you.

Employment Agencies

There are many agencies around in a whole variety of fields that specialize in hiring people for management and professional positions as well as general employees. They traditionally charge only when they have found a suitable candidate. The advantage of agencies is they are cheaper than headhunters. The disadvantage is that they can just throw bodies at you because that's how they make their commissions.

There are agencies such as Manpower, Pinstripe, and various others that will supply people on a temporary basis, whether it's to fill a requirement of one day, one week, one month, or even a year. These provide a very good solution if you need people immediately.

They usually charge by the hour, or in some cases, by the contract, with a mark-up on their hourly rate to you. For instance, they might charge you 20 per cent in addition to the wages they will pay the individual. So if they're paying someone $15.00 an hour, and the mark-up is 20 per cent, they will charge you $18.00.

ADVANTAGES AND DISADVANTAGES OF RECRUITMENT FIRMS

Advantages

- They have extensive networks and access to good people over a wide area; the quality of the candidates they present is very likely to be high.
- They do all the pre-screening and come to you with only the three to five most qualified candidates.
- They can help with compensation negotiations, offer letters, and other technical aspects of hiring.

Disadvantages

- They are expensive because they do all of the "pre-work."
- They can take some time since they are searching for high quality candidates.

10. Human Resources Development Canada

Some companies use local offices of Human Resources Development Canada to post job vacancies. While Human Resources Development Canada was known as the government service that provided notoriously poor quality candidates, their services have improved considerably over the last two or three years. They work creatively with firms to put on job fairs or list summer employment opportunities. They also provide an interactive database for jobs that is posted right across the country. Fortunately, they have shaken off the image of providing poor quality recruits and now are much more responsive to the needs of companies.

David Haslam of Presidential Plumbing Ltd. said: "When I want to attract people from other areas I place an ad with Employment Canada. The ad goes Canada-wide and there is no charge for it. It's very good because it attracts unemployed people. We are having people call now from the eastern provinces, and even as far away as New York City."

ADVANTAGES AND DISADVANTAGES OF HUMAN RESOURCES DEVELOPMENT CANADA

Advantages

- It is a free service.
- It allows you to target the kind of people you require to an extent.

Disadvantages

- Since the postings are very widely seen by a large variety of job seekers, you may get applicants who are not suitable.
- Extra time may be spent on the screening process.
- This source may not attract the potential recruits that you require.

SCREENING APPLICANTS

Screening is the process by which a large number of applications are ranked in order, from the most likely to those least likely. This allows you to eliminate some applications and permits you to interview only those candidates with the best potential for your company.

As Margaret Kerr and JoAnn Kurtz say in *Make It Legal*: "You may be flooded with applications. If that happens, you won't possibly be able to interview everyone, so you'll have to screen the applicants to decide which ones to interview. The screening process should be based on the job description and qualifications list you prepared for the job, and not on any of the grounds prohibited by human rights legislation."[2]

Sometimes a certain number of candidates who have applied but do not fit the job description can be eliminated easily at the very beginning of the process, when you are still in the paper (or Web) application stage. But true screening is more than this: it usually requires some type of personal contact with the candidate short of the formal job interview. Initial screening can be done by telephone. A telephone conversation allows you to get a sense of interests, skills, and attitudes of the applicant. Information about the company can be provided to the potential candidates, which may enable them to see if you are a fit for their needs.

Clearly, you need to think of a screening call as a miniature employment interview. Your questions must be well planned so that in a relatively brief call you can reliably qualify (or disqualify) a candidate as one of the few—usually from three to five—you wish to interview. If you don't ask the right questions, you may see the wrong candidates and dismiss the right ones, and if your screening calls are not well focused, they may squander much of the time they are meant to save.

The following chapter, "The Interview," contains a guide to questions that should be asked of potential candidates and those that shouldn't because they are prohibited by human rights legislation. This guide can be used in the screening call.

Once the screening process is complete, it is good policy and common courtesy to send a polite letter to the applicants you have eliminated at this stage, advising them that you are unable to offer them an interview. That way the applicant disqualified at the paper application stage knows that the application was at least received and considered; the applicant who was telephoned receives a follow-up response informing him/her of the results of the conversation.

THE INTERVIEW

The interview is one of the most important steps in selecting a candidate. This subject might better be called the interview process because in many cases it takes more than a single interview to complete this phase of your assessment of a candidate. This chapter discusses the common mistakes made during the interview, the preparation required for successful interviewing, questions that should and should not be asked, and the assessment of candidates.

As noted earlier, the recruitment process, and particularly the interview, should be viewed as a public relations exercise. The way potential candidates are treated during the interview tells them a great deal about the culture, values, and potential of the company. If they are treated badly, they will be unlikely to accept a job offer or refer other people to the company and may not even buy the company's products or services. On the other hand, if candidates are treated well—even if they don't get hired—they will speak well (or at least not negatively) of the company to other people.

Thinking through every aspect of the interview, and planning for it, takes time but is well worth the trouble.

THE SIX MOST COMMON INTERVIEW ERRORS

Knowing the don'ts of interviewing helps in avoiding harmful errors and provides insight into what successful interviewing should be like. The April/May 1998 issue of PROFIT magazine contained an article on errors made in the interview process.[1] The article outlines four basic errors and I have added two more. Together, they form the following checklist of the six common interviewing mistakes:

1. **Talking too much.** Many interviewers talk too much during the interview. They are proud to be part of the company and go on and on about this subject. This not only prevents them from acquiring needed information about the candidate, but it violates the important principle of finding out about the candidate first, giving information about the company later. If this order is reversed, the interviewer risks getting answers that are tailored to what he or she has revealed and are less valuable in assessing the candidate. Thus, interviewers who simply talk on and on in an interview, besides boring the candidates, run the risk of giving away important details too early.

   Talking too much might involve telling people far too much about the job and the company or talking about the interviewer's experience and not giving the interviewee a chance to get a word in edgewise about their own relevant experience or competencies.

2. **Not asking all the candidates the same questions.** It is easy to get sidetracked from a line of questioning, or to become bored with it, especially if you are on your umpteenth interview of the day. But how can you compare one candidate with another if you don't ask them all the same questions?

   An example of this could occur when the interviewers have drafted a whole list of questions but forget to take their notes with them, and end up asking one candidate one set of questions, and another candidate a whole other set. Only at the end of the process would they realize that they haven't got the same information from all the candidates. This makes it very difficult to make comparisons between them.

3. **Asking useless questions and accepting general answers.** Many questions asked by unprepared interviewers are wasteful and are often just a rehash of what is written on the candidate's résumé. It is important to use the candidate's paper application to build up a specific and detailed list of the things you want to find out more about: the things you need to know in order to determine whether this person, who looks good on paper, is the right one for your company. What distinguishes him or her from others with the same qualifications? What do you need to know about him or her that is **not** on the résumé?

An example of a useless question would be "Tell me which sports teams you are a member of." This question might have a very interesting answer, but it really does not have much to do with any particular job skills or experience you are looking for.

Avoid accepting general answers. You might ask, "Can you tell me about the specific experience you've had in working for a retail company, and what the results were that you wanted to achieve." The candidate could come back and say, "Well, I've worked for a number of stores and my results were always very good." The answer is non-specific and unacceptable, because what you want to know is which stores they've worked for, how long they worked for them, and what the exact sales results or required results were that they achieved.

4. **Losing focus.** Inexperienced interviewers tend to lose control of the process and allow the candidate to take over. Do not allow yourself to be led into off-topic discussions. Losing focus means getting off topic and talking about something that has absolutely no relevance to the interview candidate. Again, it might be talking about vacations, or sports, or asking questions about interests that have little or no bearing on the kinds of things you need to discover about the candidate.

5. **Making snap judgements.** Interviewers often make snap judgements, either positive or negative, based on such things as how the candidate looks, whether he or she came from the same area as the interviewer, or went to the same school or university. Or the candidate may simply remind the interviewer of someone else.

Making snap judgements removes the possibility of assessing "fit" in any meaningful way. Fit may seem like an intangible but in the workplace it is very real; conflict with the corporate culture is a frequent reason for employees leaving. Hiring someone you like but who does not fit is the mistake that results from snap judgements.

An example of this might result from discovering that the candidate went to the same school or university as you did. This then leads to an immediate judgement that because you went there, it's a good school, and you should therefore hire that person. In fact, they may not have the qualifications or skills that you require, so it is important to avoid making snap judgements based on appearance, common friendships, or common educational experiences.

6. **Relying on memory instead of notes.** Many interviewers fail to take notes during an interview and therefore tend to forget what each person interviewed has said. It is important to take notes during the process and to do it in an "instructive framework."

Note taking is important to help keep your memory accurate and to record each candidate's responses. Where multiple interviewers are used, notes are vital in comparing responses: how can you compare notes if you don't have any? Where a candidate may be interviewed several times (an initial interview and then a follow-up), or where a candidate may be interviewed at several levels in the company, notes are the only objective means for the interviewers to compare their responses to the candidate.

An "instructive framework" for note taking is important for these same reasons. Unless the various interviewers have comparable lists of questions, and make comparably detailed notes about the responses to each question, the combined results of the interviews will be hard to assess.

PREPARING FOR THE INTERVIEW

Preparation for the interview is vital. It is all too easy to simply turn up for the interview without having done any kind of preparation. Good preparation includes:

1. Reading the candidate's résumé and the job description in advance, noting any gaps in the résumé, preparing questions about points that are of interest to you and are important to explore.

2. Determining the questions to ask in advance.

3. Developing a framework for assessing candidates against one another.

4. Allowing enough time to meet the candidates. If you do not allow enough time for an interview, it creates a very poor impression, giving the candidate the idea that he or she is not important to you, particularly if you constantly accept phone calls and allow people to interrupt you during the interview. It is essential to give enough time so that you can properly focus on the candidate, ask the right questions, and really determine whether the person will fit in with your company.

5. Allowing for a room free from interruption. If you do not have an appropriate room—one that is free from distractions and that has suitable furniture and lighting—consider renting a meeting room in a local hotel or an office in an executive suite or in your local trade or professional association.

Asking Appropriate Questions

Asking the appropriate questions is the essence of the first three points, above. Knowing how to ask the appropriate questions is an essential part of preparation. Your questions must be carefully determined in advance to yield the information you want, everyone in the interviewing process must be on the same page about them, and you must have in place a method to assess the information the questions yield.

To properly prepare for the interview, you need to ask the same questions of all candidates. This allows you to better assess them against the same framework.

If multiple interviewers are being used, it is very important to ensure that you all agree on a framework and what areas each interviewer will cover. Also, you need to ensure that everyone provides the candidates with similar information about the company and the position that is being filled. This is true whether several interviewers talk to a candidate simultaneously or whether different interviewers each see the candidate separately.

THINGS YOU CANNOT ASK

The human rights legislation in Canada is very specific. It exists to ensure that there is no discrimination against any individual on the basis of the following points:

- Race
- Colour
- Religion
- Creed
- Gender
- Sexual orientation
- National origin
- Ancestry
- Handicap
- Record of offences
- Marital status
- Citizenship
- Age
- Family status
- Receipt of public assistance

The following areas, in general, should not be included when questioning candidates—either on the application form, in the screening call, or during the interview—because they contravene human rights legislation:

1. Marital status questions should not be asked to find out whether a person is married, has children, is pregnant, or is planning to have children.

2. Family questions that relate specifically to family size, plans for children, childcare arrangements, spouse's employment or salary

3. Age

4. National origin and anything that relates to race, colour, ancestry, ethnic origin, place of origin, or citizenship

5. Arrests

6. Convictions, unless the information bears directly on job responsibilities

7. Credit ratings or garnishments

8. Non-professional organization memberships

9. Religious and political beliefs

10. Height and weight

11. Disabilities, physical and mental, unless a certain disability will prevent the candidate from doing the job

QUESTIONS YOU CAN ASK

You are able to ask the following questions, and they will not contravene the human rights legislation. This comes under the heading of a bona fide job requirement that is acceptable within the legislation.

You would ask these questions if they related to the job requirements and the specific job duties and skills that an individual requires to do the job.

1. Are you legally entitled to work in Canada?

2. Are you available to travel out of town or overnight?

3. Would you be willing to relocate?

4. Are you licensed to drive a vehicle?

5. Is there anything that would prevent you from being at work from 8 a.m. until 4 p.m., for instance?

6. Is there anything that would prevent you from working overtime?

7. Is there anything that would prevent you from lifting heavy weights? (The interviewer will need to talk specifically about the weights that will be lifted and the frequency of the lifting.)

8. Is there anything to prevent you from sitting for long periods of time?

Competency, Character, and Fit

When you interview a prospective employee, you are trying to find out if that person:

- has the skills and competency required to do the job
- will be honest and reliable
- can take direction or work independently as needed
- will fit in with the culture and be easy to work with

In order to discover if the candidate has these qualities, you may ask questions to find out what they have done before, about the kinds of skills they have demonstrated, and about previous employment: what they did, how they did it, their previous accomplishments, and the results they achieved.

Of course, these topics will have been covered in the candidate's application and résumé. The purpose of the interview is to use what you have read and go beyond it by asking specific questions that change written qualifications into a clear sense of the person's actual performance and personality. You can also ask candidates about their current career plans and what opportunities they want for growth, development, and advancements. As well, you can ask them about education and interests if these are applicable.

As we've suggested, you do need to ask all candidates the same questions; however, you will need some flexibility because you may need more information from some candidates in particular areas than others. For instance, if some part of a candidate's résumé is rather thin with regard to the kind of experience they have in the field you're looking for, you may want to probe a lot more deeply into this particular area.

On the other hand, there may be some areas you won't need to ask too many questions about, for instance, culture fit. You may get the idea immediately that this kind of person's demeanour and the way they are responding to the questions will fit in with the company a lot more readily than the other candidates. You may want to spend less time exploring fit and teamwork than you would with other candidates. The whole issue is to have a common framework and cover all the relevant points, but to use judgement and flexibility in terms of probing more deeply on some questions and less on others.

In the case of high-achieving people or workers with skills in hot fields, determining what they want is vital in attracting and retaining them. Giving the impression that you want to know because you want to communicate and accommodate is the first step. The second is to use the knowledge you have gained at the interview to make an attractive offer to the candidate you wish to hire.

Technical Requirements

If this is a technical position, and the first recruiter or interviewer is not entirely familiar with the job, it is important to set up two to three crucial technological questions with someone in the company who understands the technology, and to get the answers from that person. The interviewer can do a better pre-screening if he or she is easily able to ask and get appropriate answers relating to technical skills. Of course, with such candidates a second and more specifically technical interview is likely to be required.

Creating Rapport with the Candidate

This may not strictly be part of preparation for the interview, but it is good to think in advance about how you will create rapport. It is important to put candidates at ease in order to avoid nervousness and produce an environment that will encourage confidence and communication. This involves small talk such as personal introductions and conversation about their journey, the weather, or perhaps some interesting current event, as a means to get the interview process going. It also involves, as mentioned above, having an appropriate office that is comfortable and free from interruptions.

The Interview Schedule

During the process it is important to limit the number of candidates to no more than three or four a day: more than that makes it difficult for most interviewers to remain positive and upbeat. Also, you may find that one candidate begins to blur into another.

Generally, interviewers should allow an hour per candidate for each interview, and allow half an hour afterwards to reflect and make notes regarding the strengths and weaknesses of the candidate just interviewed. It's useful to have gaps in between interviews during the course of the day, because, as noted above, candidates may begin to blur into each other in the interviewer's mind.

THE INTERVIEW ITSELF

There are two basic secrets to interviewing:

1. Ask candidates to give examples of specific events in which they have used their skills and competencies.
2. Avoid asking "close-ended" questions with yes/no answers.

Using these two things will unlock conversation and reveal the information you need.

Event Interviewing: Getting Specifics from Candidates

Close-ended questions will kill conversation, whereas open-ended questions cause it to flow. "Are you reliable?" is an example of a close-ended question; it would simply elicit the answer "Yes."

To get fuller information, you need to ask some specific questions about specific events. For example, if you wanted to find out if a person was reliable, you would ask for an example of a time when he or she handled a crisis or some event that demonstrates that he or she is reliable.

This kind of question could be, "Do you have a diploma related to this particular field?" The answer might be, "Yes." You would frame this question by saying, "What did you study at college?" That way, the candidate cannot simply answer "yes," but must tell you in some detail what they studied, and what diploma they received.

Another example might be, "Have you worked for a similar kind of company?" This is also a "close-ended" question and could simply receive a "yes" or "no" response. It would be better to rephrase the question, "Tell me about other similar organizations you've worked for." This would avoid the simple "yes/no" answer.

Asking specific questions means asking the candidate to:

• give an example

• describe the situation and the circumstances

• discuss how he or she handled the situation

• discuss the outcome

You need to do this event interviewing, as it is called, in many areas for each candidate. For instance, if you want to know how a candidate improved sales in a previous position, you can ask the same kinds of questions: ask the candidate to give an example, provide a circumstance, discuss how it was handled, and the outcome. Such questions should also be asked with regard to particular traits you are searching for such as customer focus, teamwork, creativity, motivating people.

Covering the Bases

Your preparation should have made you very aware of the most important qualities you need in the person you are trying to hire: skills, competencies, personality traits, experience, and the like. It is a good idea to have several questions designed to elicit specifics under each area that is important to you.

Control the Interview

During the course of the interview, it is essential to maintain control of the interview situation. Don't lose focus. Take notes and make sure you do not allow candidates to stray into areas of discussion not directly related to the job. Be flexible enough to follow up leads that occur during the conversation: don't over-prepare to the extent that you are afraid of departing from your pre-arranged script.

Avoid straying into areas not relating to the job. For example, if you find out that you both worked for the same company at one time, do not go into a long discussion regarding people you know in common and generally catching up on local gossip and information about that company. This might be very interesting but it can eat into the time of the interview and may not reveal information about what the candidate did and what their strengths and weaknesses are.

Remember to ask candidates questions about their past first, and only afterwards provide information about the company. If you tell them a lot about the company and the position first, they may quickly restructure their answers and tell you what you want to hear. It is better to ask them about themselves: what they've done, how well they've done it, and what kind of results they've got.

Telling Candidates about the Company

Presumably you are only interviewing candidates whose applications have already been screened; in other words, applicants you are quite interested in. That means you will have to be prepared to give them sufficient information, preferably in the last part of the interview, about the position and the company. It is important to elicit their responses to this information and their demands or wishes: this is knowledge you need to structure an offer that will attract a candidate you want to hire.

Kieran O'Briain of Kee Transport made a special point of this aspect of interviewing. "The term we use, actually printed on our business card, is: 'Your goals are our priority.' Which means exactly what it says. All we really have to do is determine what the goals of applicants are and then help them achieve those goals. If we can't assist them in achieving those goals, we can't hire them."

Multiple Interviewers

The use of multiple interviewers is a good idea because it:

- prevents personal bias
- allows the candidate to get a good idea of what the company is like and the type of people in it
- allows both candidate and interviewer to determine if that person will fit with the culture

Interviewers could include the candidate's potential supervisor, peers, and the people who will be working for him or her. However, when you are using multiple interviewers you must plan for efficiency and speed. You cannot allow scheduling conflicts and the like to drag out the process of interviewing a candidate. As I've noted before, it is important that interviews happen quickly, particularly in a hot market, because the best candidates may well find jobs with other companies if you delay.

Susan Niczowski of Summer Fresh Salads Inc. told me that she often hires candidates directly from within her company or through a recruitment firm and then uses a multiple interviewer process: "We'll go through their résumés initially, and I usually narrow it down to about five people. Then I try to interview three of them, and look at the pluses and the minuses. After that I bring in my sister, who's the plant manager, and the two of us decide who will fit our team.

"Each department has its own supervisor or lead hand, and if we're hiring people in that department, I'll have that particular supervisor interview and then he or she will double-check with me and we'll see if that particular person fits the mould."

ASSESSMENT AND SELECTION

After the various interviews have taken place, selection of the final candidates can be made. It is important to have more than one final candidate, since reference checks may reveal information that eliminates a person. In assessing one candidate against another, use your list of the areas that are really important to you: skills, competencies, personality traits, experience, and other criteria particularly relevant to the company. Assess each candidate at the end of the interview on a scale of one to five against each of these key criteria.

Also, make notes on each candidate at the end of the interview. Remember, notes are useful for you as you begin to compare one candidate against another. They are especially important if you are using multiple interviewers. In selecting the final candidate, use the numerical assessments and comments from all interviewers recording their immediate impression of each interview. Also use the notes taken by each interviewer during the process, plus consultation with the interviewers, to add the stage of "sober second thought."

In her remarks quoted above, Susan Niczowski describes a collegial process of interviewing and assessment in which she, as chief executive, makes the final decision. This is ideal. If you have ensured that colleagues and people who will work with the new person have had a hand in the hiring process, especially the interviewing, your final choice will be easier to make and more secure.

REFERENCE CHECKS AND THE OFFER LETTER

Reference checking is an extremely important aspect of the hiring process, because if it is done inadequately it can lead to mistakes in hiring that can cost you dearly. That is the point of an incident narrated to me by David Anderson of CANATOM NPM.

The company had recruited an individual to expedite parts being manufactured for an offshore client. "He was filing reports to us about the processing of the parts," David explained, "which were in fact a figment of his imagination, and unknowingly we were passing these on to the client. We found out later that he hadn't even visited clients or manufacturers. He would just make up reports to say that he had been there. Eventually this caught up with him. When the delivery did not come through on time the client wanted to know why they had not been warned beforehand. We hadn't told them, because we did not know there was a problem."

He continues, "The moral of this story is that we should have picked up this problem during the hiring stage because it turned out that his references had not been fully checked. The two references he had given provided glowing testimonials. If all you get are good references you have to be careful of the source."

> W hen asked to provide references, most candidates will only provide names of people they know will give them a good report. It's therefore important to try and find other ways to check a candidate's reference. You can call people you know in the same company or Industry and ask whether they know the individual and what they think about them. This is a quick and informal way of doing things and often yields far more factual information about the candidate than going solely by references. If you've developed a good rapport with people in an agency, you could ask them if they've heard of the person and what their general impressions are.

HOW TO CHECK REFERENCES

This incident highlights the care necessary in checking references and the difficulties that can be involved. It is important not to accept only the reference letters or testimonials provided by the candidate as part of his or her application. Instead, you should also check other features of the person's record and have some direct conversations by telephone with previous employers, educational institutions, and the like.

A prospective employee can write anything in a résumé or on a job application, and say anything (quite convincingly) in a job interview, and turn out to be a liar. So check references to confirm an applicant's qualifications and employment history.

> An adequate reference check would include the following:
>
> - Contact educational institutions and licensing bodies to confirm that the applicant has the credentials claimed.
> - Telephone past employers to confirm the period of employment, positions held, duties performed, and compensation received.

In terms of reference checks, schools and colleges will give out information over the phone. They will tell you that a person did attend the school, what years they were there and how long they were in attendance. They will also confirm any designation or qualification they received.

Past employers are particularly important in reference checks. As with the employment interview itself, you should be ready with a few specific questions that will elicit the information you need. You should also ask former employers about:

• the quality of the applicant's work

• the applicant's ability to get along well with others

• whether the applicant had a good attitude and was motivated

• the applicant's honesty

• the reason the applicant left that job

• whether the past employer would hire the applicant again

In terms of past employers, they usually will tell you that the person did work for the company and the period of employment, as well as the positions held. Many are reluctant to give information pertaining to the good or bad points of the person because they may feel they could be slandering or libelling the individual.

It is unfair to call current employers because that lets them know their employee is looking for another job. I would not recommend calling the current employer.

With regard to past employers, it is permissible to ask specific questions. You can ask a previous employer about the quality of the applicant's work. You would ask them about what the applicant did in relation to the kind of work you require them to do, how well they did it, and what results they achieved. In terms of asking about the applicant's ability to get along with other people, you can ask for examples of how they were a team player and how they helped out other employees in the company when they got in a jam. You can also ask about the employee's attitude and motivation by asking for examples of their going beyond the call of duty in completing a particular task.

You can ask why, in their opinion, the applicant left the job. Don't press too much on this one because there may be areas the employer may not want to get into. If the individual was fired, they can tell you that, but this is one area where it is quite difficult to probe too deeply. But you can ask if the employer would hire the applicant again, and you might say, for example, "If that particular kind of position, or the same position, opened up again would you take the individual back?"

Whether the previous employer would hire the applicant again can be an essential question, giving you a sense of whether the person truly is highly valued or whether the employer is simply giving a hand to someone he doesn't mind doing without.

When asking questions about an applicant's competency and experience, ask the person giving the reference to provide a specific behavioural example. In other words, use "event interviewing," just as in the employment interview itself. For instance, if you need to know about the applicant's experience in sales, ask about what sales he or she made, the process used to get the sale, the difficulties encountered, and the results obtained.

PROBATIONARY PERIODS AND CONTRACTS

The above presents the ideal case. It is not always possible to check references as fully as should be done, particularly since sources of information are not always forthcoming and sincere, and since the culture of some industries does not permit accurate checking.

In such situations, it is beneficial to hire the individual for a probationary or contract period to test the compatibility of a person with your company. When you're employing a person full time, it's always a good idea to specify a period of time, say three to six months, during which you will put the person on probation and decide whether they meet your expectations or are a good fit with your culture. This makes it clear that if at the end of that time the candidate does not work out, their employment will be terminated.

A contract position, on the other hand, can be offered when you have a job for a certain period of time, say two months or six months, in which you want a project finished. You then make it quite clear to the individual that at the end of that period (unless the contract has to be extended for some reason) the employment will end. Therefore, a contract position is for a given time and with very clear expectations of when the person's contract employment will end.

David Haslam of Presidential Plumbing Ltd. gives a vivid picture of the difficulties that often exist in reference checking. "We really don't have the same avenues that corporate people have when they're calling around for references or really looking at a résumé. I would say that 80 per cent of the people that we're hiring today do not even submit résumés. They'll say they worked for other people. With the mentality that's in my industry, it's impossible to call your competition and ask how an employee was. They'll say he was terrible. They will lie to you. They're really not in it to help you. You're direct competition. So, they're not interested in telling you.

"So essentially what you have to do is, you have to hire a person, and try him out. You have to hire him on a trial period."

It is not only in industries and situations where full reference checking is impossible that trial periods and contracts are a good idea. Even though references are checked and all necessary precautions are taken, the person hired still may prove not to be a good fit for the position or the company. The way to avoid costly mistakes and terminations is to hire a person for a probationary period or on a contract basis. You can decide at the end of this specified period whether to hire that individual or end the relationship.

If you intend to use a probation or contract to check suitability, this, of course, must be part of the job description given to the candidates. It does not have to appear in a brief advertisement, but it must appear in any printed or Web site material offering a full description of the position, and it must be stated clearly in the latter portion of the interview, when you talk to the candidate about the company and the position. This "no surprises" approach is part of the principle of communication, of presenting a culture that will attract the best people.

THE JOB OFFER

Making a job offer should always be done in person, or at least by telephone, but never by letter. The job offer should be made to the individual in such a way that the details of the position, responsibilities, salary and bonuses, benefits, and vacations can be explained. There are a number of reasons why this is important. First, to begin establishing personal contact, the offer should always be made by the person for whom the individual will be working. Second, it allows the candidate to ask questions and clarify points about the offer. If you can't make the offer in person, which sometimes is unavoidable, at the very least, do it by telephone.

This personal and informal first stage does have to be followed up with an offer letter.

The Offer Letter

The offer letter formalizes your offer of employment. Once again, make sure that there are no surprises: the letter formally offering the job to the candidate must describe the position as advertised, described in your company's material, and discussed with the successful applicant in the interview.

The offer letter should:

- State the commencement date.

- Describe the terms and conditions of employment (work hours, travel, etc.).

- Give details of the salary, benefits, holidays and vacation allowance, and bonuses, including any incentives, profit sharing, or other instruments that have been agreed upon.

- Outline the probationary period, if one is being used.

- Set expectations and, if a probationary period is being used, expectations deliverable at the end of that time. These should include the expectations on both sides: what the new hire owes to the company and what the company owes in response if the employee fulfils the expectations.

- Include a non-competition agreement if necessary. That is an agreement by which the employee promises not to work for the competition during and after employment with you for a predetermined length of time.

Follow-Up

Once the candidate has accepted, you will need to open a personnel file for the new recruit, and ensure that he or she is put on the payroll of the company. Also ensure that the new hire has all the tools and facilities needed to do the job. If all is in readiness as soon as the person arrives for the first day of work, he or she will feel professionally treated and welcome.

As soon as possible after a hire has been made, you should notify the unsuccessful candidates by mail.

Successfully welcoming a new hire into your company will maximize mutual respect and the prospect for retaining the employee. It is a process that begins the moment the employee is hired and is essentially a part of the whole hiring process. However, it belongs basically with strategies to retain the employee, which are the subject of Part Four, "Development," and will be dealt with in the first chapter of that section, Chapter 12, "Good Communications and New Employee Orientation."

COMPENSATION

Don't model your compensation program on someone else's. Your circumstances are unique, so tailor the program to meet your specific needs.

—Ellie Maggio, William M. Mercer Ltd.

Does your company's success depend on your ability to outbid your competitors, dollar for dollar, for each new hire? What are people really working for? Do you feel caught between the contradictions of Canada's high unemployement rate and a lack of skilled workers you need to meet customer demand? Chapters 8 to 11 examine the crucial question of salaries, benefits, and incentives, an area of particular concern for small businesses which must find means to compete for prime candidates with companies that are larger and richer than themselves.

CHAPTER EIGHT

PAY:
WHO GETS WHAT?

Paying people is a simple thing to consider but a very complex thing to do right. You have to pay people in order to attract them to your company and to retain them. Not many of us are willing to work for free! The complexity of compensation lies in the need to know *what* to pay both new and existing employees and *how* to pay them. Compensation needs to be affordable for the business while at the same time ensuring that good quality people are attracted and retained. It also needs to be structured so as to ensure that the efforts of employees are directed to achieving the company's goals.

This chapter's purpose is to detail the elements of payment for new hires. However, we begin by reviewing and adding new insights to some of the material covered in Chapter 2, "Attracting and Retaining the Right People," because it is crucial to coordinate compensation-as-payment with other factors.

As we showed in Chapter 2, money is not the sole motivation for someone deciding to work for a company, whether it is large or small. Karen Flavelle of Purdy's Chocolates believes money can "de-motivate" if it's not competitive, but by itself, it isn't a real motivator. "Working through frustrations and finding solutions is what makes people happy in their work."

Chapter 2 brought out that pay must be competitive, but often small businesses are not able to outdo large firms in a head-to-head bidding war on salary and benefits. So compensation, to work for you, must be competitive but it must also be just one part of a total self-marketing approach that your company makes to good job candidates, emphasizing the company's overall culture. Entrepreneurial and other small to medium-size businesses have other advantages to offer in tempting and motivating high achievers.

HOW CAN SMALL COMPANIES COMPETE FOR THE BEST PEOPLE?

Small companies often see themselves at a disadvantage in that they cannot afford to pay as much as large corporations. They feel this makes it difficult to attract and keep staff, particularly in a tight job market. The thing to do is to stress other aspects of the company in conjunction with the level of pay it offers. For instance, some people want to go to work in an organization that they feel aligns with their values; almost everyone is familiar with the success stories, such as The Body Shop or Ben and Jerry's, that grew from tiny roots by attracting both personnel and customers through this "values" appeal.

In the high-tech organization, which normally has a younger workforce, employees often want a sense of ownership in the organization. They want stock options so that they can get rich like Bill Gates. But another factor that is just as important (and even more so for some powerful individuals) is the desire to be on the leading edge where the scientific or technological action is. Employees motivated in this way will often take less pay if they believe in the future of the organization, the type of work it has to offer, and the chance to be in on the development of "the next big thing."

These are just three of the things that the small firm can use when trying to attract good job candidates. As discussed in

Chapter 2, there are many small business advantages that supplement or even outweigh the question of compensation pure and simple.

THINGS SMALL BUSINESS CAN OFFER

- a sense of membership in the company
- values-based business goals and practices, and the chance for the employee to work in alignment with his or her values
- stock option plans offering a sense of ownership
- a chance to make a difference in an advanced field
- supportive and effective management that is flexible and recognizes and encourages the talent and contribution of all the employees
- challenging opportunities to learn about a new technology or business processes
- exposure to a wide variety of work
- promotion opportunities
- interesting projects with chances to use creativity and develop leadership skills and credentials
- accomplishment acknowledged by titles to quickly reflect the outstanding person's level of achievement

Crucial as it is to understand and use the total approach to attracting new hires, this still leaves the questions of what and how to pay people, the subject of this chapter.

THE COMPONENTS OF A COMPENSATION STRATEGY

Ellie Maggio of William M. Mercer Ltd. comments, "I think employers are trying to be a lot more strategic about how they package their total compensation package. So they're really trying to pull it all together, not just saying you're going to be paid a base pay of X and an incentive of Y. They bring the whole package together."

This is due to changing conditions in the contemporary labour market, and small businesses can take advantage of these changes. Ellie continues, "The bigger portion of the total compensation package is becoming variable in nature, so most organizations are trying to be competitive or even lagging slightly on the base pay side. The incentives component is taking a bigger portion of their pay. These incentives are often based on qualitative factors like customer satisfaction and some sort of key project completion or milestone accomplishment." Maggio means that base pay these days is relatively small in relation to variable pay, which includes stock options, bonuses, and group RSPs. The variable pay is very much dependent on the profitability and success of the organization.

Widespread acknowledgement and acceptance of these trends, by owners and workers alike, give you the latitude to pay a little less on the base pay end and structure an attractive compensation package, using incentives, around the profit level of the new hire's performance for your company. In essence you can pay new hires out of what they bring in to your business.

This leads us to a rule that should be kept in mind. If we divide compensation into pay, incentives, and benefits, pay and benefits must be competitive but it is incentives that are likely to be the driver in attracting and retaining the best people for the small business. So the three elements must be considered and structured together.

From her experience and analysis of small business human resources needs, Ellie Maggio suggested the following checklist of dos and don'ts for compensation:

- ❑ Be strategic. Know what the market is paying, and how to keep your compensation ahead of, or in line with, other companies in the market.
- ❑ Provide opportunities for growth. Ensure that some of your employees have the opportunity to learn new skills and be part of bigger projects.
- ❑ Have a very good understanding of who your workforce is, what they want, and what they need.
- ❑ Know as much as there is to know about each of the employee groups in your company, and set some of the pay package around that.
- ❑ Tailor your own unique compensation program that is appropriate for your circumstances. Do not try to copy someone else.

We can synthesize these insights into six basic components to a total compensation strategy:

1. What to pay new hires

2. Giving perks in the form of cash and non-cash bonuses

3. Having performance-linked bonuses and incentives

4. Giving opportunities for profit sharing and stock options

5. Providing health and dental insurance

6. Setting up pension plans and group RRSPs

These components will be reviewed in this chapter and the next two, to provide a complete account of the key aspects of compensation for small and medium-size enterprises. This chapter looks at the issue of what to pay new hires (component 1). Chapter 9, "Incentives," covers the different types of incentives that can be used (components 2 to 4). Chapter 10, "Benefits," considers the types of health and dental insurance and pension plans that can be used (components 5 and 6).

WHAT TO PAY NEW HIRES

Knowing what to pay new hires is critical to any business, but to the small business entrepreneur the difference between paying too much and too little can be crucial. Too often, job pricing is done haphazardly or hastily, without enough consideration given to:

- the value of the job to the organization
- up-to-date information about the going rate for the type of job
- relationship of pay scales within the organization
- base salary as part of a compensation package including benefits and non-cash incentives

The value of the job to the organization means looking at which jobs require extra pay because it is especially important that the organization be able to attract and retain candidates for them.

Up-to-date information about the going rate for the type of job means making sure that wages, salaries, and bonuses are in line with what other people in the sector or in similar industries are paying for that particular job.

Relationship of pay scales within the organization means having a company-wide policy that ensures that those doing substantially the same job in different divisions are paid the same, and that new hires are not paid more than veterans simply because the market got hotter.

Base salary is part of a compensation package including benefits and non-cash incentives. This means making sure that you're not giving cash remuneration only when your competitors are including benefits and non-cash incentives as part of their compensation package, and candidates are going to other organizations because of them.

Ellie Maggio suggests that when a company is starting up it must do some market pay research. There are two basic ways to do such research, she explains.

- They would purchase published surveys from consulting firms or various associations.

- They would retain somebody's services to conduct a custom survey, which would be a survey of base pay, incentive pay, and compensation design issues for their comparative organizations or competitors.

There are various ways to get information and research about pay. You can contact consulting firms who specialize in compensation. This can be done through the Yellow Pages or by getting referrals. You can also go to your local Boards of Trade, Chambers of Commerce, and trade organizations to find out who they would go to for published surveys. These surveys can range anywhere from $300 to $5,000, depending on the nature of the request and the kinds of jobs for which you want the data.

In terms of retaining someone's services to conduct a survey, this is a more expensive proposition, particularly if you go to one of the larger compensation companies. My advice would be to find an independent consultant who specializes in compensation and contract their services. This needs to be done carefully. Again, the cost can range anywhere from $500 up, depending on the amount of time you're actually buying. Please refer to Chapter 19 on the hiring of consultants to see how this is done.

But market research alone is not enough to base pay scales on, Ellie points out. "There has to be some sort of corporate philosophy on how you're going to pay compensation. It's one thing to learn what the market's paying, and it's quite another thing to decide how you're going to pay your people. Ask yourself whether you are going to lead the market, whether you're just going to be competitive, or whether in fact you might lag the market for certain jobs where you can afford some turnover."

Some Entrepreneurs Speak

How and why Canada's most successful small business executives decide on what to pay workers varies widely, underlining the truth of Ellie Maggio's rule that every situation is unique, so you can't just base your compensation program on what others are doing. The following anecdotes illustrate this diversity through the experiences from industries as diverse as personal aesthetics, nuclear power, plumbing, food processing and sales, and trucking.

Mabel Jakimtschuk, owner-operator of Sherwood Village Spa, takes an informal approach to setting pay scales. "I more or less know the salary where people feel comfortable," she says. "Most of the time when I hire people, I ask them for their expected salary. And then I go from there." Mabel gives them a three-month probation period, "and then we just move the salaries up, based on their performance. I also pay commission on the retail products sold. It's a motivation for them to increase their income."

Interestingly, a number of the people I interviewed deliberately pay above the average or median market rates, for a variety of reasons.

"We have a set of pay scales," says David Anderson of CANATOM NPM. "We have a set of job families, job descriptions, and we need to have some structure and relativity of those pay scales with both the market place and with our parent companies. Since a significant percentage of our employees are engineers, we follow very closely what the engineering profession is doing in the provinces where we employ these engineers. So we use those as yardsticks to establish our pay scales, and then we have a sort of general policy that we will maintain our scales in the upper quartile."

This is because, says Anderson, one of CANATOM NPM's core values and beliefs is that the company's people are its most important resource and that "our clients will get the highest quality products and services. You aren't going to be able to do that if you have compensations that are in the lower quartile, because you'll get the people you deserve."

David Haslam of Presidential Plumbing Ltd. has a non-unionized firm that services construction sites and major renovations. "In my industry, the way I can attract people is by offering them a higher wage than the competition, or even the union will offer."

"I feel that you only get out what you put into something," says Susan Niczowski of Summer Fresh Salads Inc. "We like to be thought of as middle to the high end, and basically, when we've done our surveys within the food industry, our rate of pay is actually quite high compared to the others." She says her surveys are informal; for example, asking headhunters to see what people in the industry are paying.

But sometimes there are economic dangers in paying too high a rate. Kieran O'Briain, whose company Kee Transport supplies drivers to trucking companies, talks about one competitor that raised its pay rates to drivers by nearly 40 per cent in order to attract the best drivers. "But I don't think you have to go to that kind of extreme. I mean, paying a premium over everybody else may work for a while, but eventually the rest of the industry will catch up," Kieran says.

Finding Out What the Market Is Paying

There are several sources of information available to small firms that will help them with decisions on what to pay:

- custom surveys conducted by consultants
- broader surveys published by consulting firms
- personal networks
- trade union handbooks
- professional associations' published rates (for engineers and others)
- employment agencies

- industry and trade publications
- industry and trade associations
- boards of trade/chambers of commerce
- the Statistics Canada Web site
- job advertisements in the newspapers

To review the above points: Some of the major compensation consulting firms conduct surveys of specific job categories or industries, for example, computer and information services professionals. Also, senior management is an area for which custom surveys are widely used.

Consulting firms, such as William M. Mercer, Hewitt and Associates, and Wyatt Watson, produce general surveys for all types of jobs.

Personal networks simply means asking your colleagues and friends, and people you know with similar types of business, what they pay for particular jobs.

Trade union handbooks publish the rates for the jobs within their particular union.

Professional associations (for engineers and others) publish suggested rates for various types of tasks.

Employment agencies will often tell you the going rate for jobs.

Industry and trade associations publish rates relating to their particular areas.

Your local board of trade/chamber of commerce will have access to compensation information and can steer you to other sources.

The Statistics Canada Web site is particularly useful because it has rates for virtually every job classification in the country and is broken down geographically. The joy of this one is that the information is free and readily available.

Job ads in the newspapers are useful because they sometimes publish the going rates for particular jobs.

Published surveys will tell you base rates of pay and the types of incentives that are being offered. It must be noted that these surveys vary widely in what they will cost to buy. For instance, surveys published by the Metropolitan Toronto Board of Trade cover several categories of employees and are available for between $350 and $500 each. On the other hand, a custom market study of 30 job categories for a company with about 100 employees, conducted by a consulting firm, would cost in the $7,000 to $10,000 range. Thus, the new company has to decide how much it can afford, and where is the best place to find the information it wants.

Some of the people interviewed made extensive use of material that is readily available at little or no cost. Examples of this are noted below.

Most trades, especially where workers are unionized, have published rates. David Haslam of Presidential Plumbing Ltd. says, "There's the union book, so we know what the wages are, whether it's an hourly wage, or whether it's what we call a piece-work wage, which is more of a set price by contract. In the plumbing industry, we have a fixture price that we offer and naturally it has to compete with the union companies, essentially to attract and also maintain our people."

The trucking industry also publishes pay rates. "Everybody publishes their rates," says Kieran O'Briain of Kee Transport, "so it's not very hard to find out. There is some upward pressure on rates these days," he continues. "Some of my customers are quite profitable, and I'm in the process of trying to convince them to become leaders in the market." Kieran figures this will help him attract the drivers on the one hand, and help his customers attract new business.

The one area Kieran admits he has difficulty getting a handle on is his management staff. "That's where I could probably use an outside survey," he says. "Never having worked in an office, never having done budgets, I don't know what a receptionist should be getting. When I tell my customers what I pay my clerical staff, they keep telling me I'm overpaying, yet my staff says I'm not!"

Kieran's dilemma is not unusual. How should he sort this out? He can ask other business owners in his industry or area to tell him what they pay office and clerical staff. He can, as he states, get a consultant to do a survey for him, and he can do that by asking local boards of trade or chambers of commerce to recommend a consultant to him. He's a member of the Ontario Trucking Association, and they will probably have the kind of information he needs if he doesn't want to use a consultant.

They could tell him what he should be paying a receptionist and clerical staff in his particular business and geographical area.

Ensuring Competitive Pay

In order to retain your new hires, it is important to keep their pay competitive and up to date once they are on board.

Ellie Maggio suggests that the following five steps be used to keep pay competitive.

1. To keep pay up to date, adjust the base pay more than once a year. Traditionally most organizations review their pay scales annually. Especially if your company employs skills that are in short supply and in a hot market, these adjustments need to be made more than once a year. Employees will learn quickly of rising pay rates for their skills in other firms.

2. Ensure that new hires are not paid more than the people you hired a few months ago. If you really want to make people angry, get this one wrong.

3. Start hiring mid-range. Most of us are familiar with pay ranges that are plus or minus 20 per cent or 50 per cent. If you are looking for a hot skill, it is virtually impossible to hire at the bottom of the pay range, 20 per cent below the market competitive rate. In all probability, for most positions you are going to be hiring pretty close to the market rate for the job.

4. Anything you do that adds to base salary above those market competitive rates better have a good value for the organization. After all, the business has to be kept profitable. You have to make sure that what you are doing in the pay package still allows the organization to have competitive rates for its products and services.

5. Make sure that pay increases are based on the results of performance reviews, as well as on market conditions.

INCENTIVES

A recent survey in PROFIT magazine showed that bonuses, profit sharing, and stock options are the main ways used to reward key employees by past PROFIT 100 winners. Companies participating in the survey said that salary should form about 65 to 76 per cent of total compensation, with the balance coming from performance-related incentives.[1] Incentives are critical to retain those employees who are essential to the company's success. Management needs to recognize who these vital contributors are and make sure they know that they are valued.

However, performance-related incentives do not appeal to all employees. As David Anderson of CANATOM NPM notes, many of the people he employs, "like the risk/reward side of the equation. But there are others who want more certainty in their life and want to know that they're going to get salary X. They don't want the degree of challenge where they may be asked to do something one day that they've never done before and would see that as a threat rather than an opportunity."

When CANATOM NPM does a job for a client for a fixed price regardless of the time it takes, they sometimes pay the people they hire on a project or contract basis. "Under those conditions," David says, "we can then hire somebody for a project on a contract. We can include a risk/reward equation in there, and we can say, we'll establish a rate at X. We'll pay you, let's say for the sake of argument, 70 per cent of X on a regular basis, and the other 30 per cent will be earnable on achieving various things that we can tie to that individual's scope of work." The rest of the company's personnel are full-time and on salary, with a profit-sharing bonus scheme for the principal officers.

This indicates that a company may need to have a group of incentive programs, some of which are performance-related to stimulate the more creative and adventurous employee, others of which are more generally related to the company's overall success to appeal to the employee more concerned with security.

EIGHT CHARACTERISTICS OF SUCCESSFUL INCENTIVE PLANS

1. **Clarity:** Every incentive plan must clearly spell out the goal that needs to be achieved, whether it is higher profits, new clients, or greater market share. It is also important to establish a clear appraisal process for any award or bonus system.

2. **Employee Involvement:** Involve employees in the design of the plan, or they will be unlikely to commit to it.

3. **Influence:** Make sure that the results required to reach the established goals can be influenced by employees. It is difficult to get enthusiastic about things that you can't influence or have some control over.

4. **Attainability:** Ensure that the goals are possible. If the bar is set too high, employees may not even try.

5. **Simplicity:** A good incentive plan allows employees to track their progress easily and calculate their rewards. Aim for two or three measurable goals at most.

6. **Publicity:** Employees need to know that the plan exists, and what they have to do to be awarded the incentive. Communicating the plan is vital to its success.

7. **Renewal:** Review and revise incentive plans regularly to ensure they still support your business objectives.

8. **Affordability:** The company must be able to bear the cost of the plan.

Bonuses, depending on the market, are typically paid on an annual basis. However, in very hot markets—those where people move easily from one job to another—bonuses may be paid quarterly. Sales people, for example, are often paid quarterly bonuses. Some companies give bonuses when a project is completed, as we note later in the chapter.

DIFFERENT TYPES OF INCENTIVE PROGRAMS

There are many different types of incentive programs. The ones noted below are the most widely used:

1. Profit Sharing

2. Project Milestone and Completion Bonuses

3. Special Awards

4. Employee Share Programs and Stock Options

1. Profit Sharing

Profit sharing occurs when companies decide to share a certain portion of their profits, say 10 per cent, with all employees. Profit-sharing plans provide bonuses to employees based on a percentage of the company profit. Obviously, for the employees to receive a bonus, the company has to make a profit! The prime advantage of profit sharing is that it makes employees feel that their work is appreciated; it also makes them focus on revenues and expenses.

As a rule, profit-sharing bonuses are paid out once a year and can be given in the form of cash or on a deferred basis.

Cash Schemes

Cash schemes are popular for a number of reasons:

• The reward is tangible and immediate.

• Employees have freedom of choice over how they use the cash.

• These schemes are easy to install and communicate.

However, from a tax perspective, if cash is given it is taxed in the hands of the employee as income received in the year it is received. Whether giving a bonus, salary, or cash, there is no difference in terms of taxation. They are all taxed in the same way and at the same rate. So it becomes a question of determining which is the most motivational form of bonus for the employer to give the employee.

Deferred Schemes

Under a deferred pay-out plan, an employee's share of company profits is placed in a trust fund and distributed at a later date. Distribution usually takes place on the employee's employment retirement, termination, or death.

The most widely used deferred plan is the group Registered Retirement Savings Plan. In these, both the employee contributions and annual earnings of the fund are exempt from the employee's taxable income until the employee actually receives the benefits. Group RSPs are the same as individual RRSPs, except that individuals pay into the company's group scheme rather than their own individual plan. Usually, the contributions are shared between the employee and the employer. In other words, the employer may also pay into the Group RSP and in some cases, may make all the contributions. This is a great scheme for the individual because they receive a contribution to their RRSP without having to pay the full amount themselves.

The advantages of deferred plans are:

- They reinforce the employee's efforts with the long-term success of the company.

- The value of the fund can be rapidly built up over time.

- Tax is deferred until the employee receives the income at a later date.

They reinforce the employee's efforts with the long-term success of the company, because the individual will see that their pay-out of cash or shares is dependent on the success of the company in the future. Thus, they are more likely to make sure that their own and others' efforts are directed toward its long-term success.

The value of the fund can be built up rapidly over time. This means that as the company becomes successful, the value of the shares can increase. Or, equally, investments of money in a good fund or account means that interest can accrue and the fund itself will increase in value.

Tax is deferred until the employee receives the income at a later date. This may be at a defined date when the shares are paid out, say in five years' time, or when the employee leaves the company.

David Howe of Eckler Partners Ltd. suggests that it is best for a small company to set up a group RRSP to which only the employees contribute. As the company becomes more profitable and has more cash available, it might then consider matching employee contributions to the fund.

Insurance companies, banks, and mutual funds will set up group RRSPs for companies. (Some of these institutions may not issue a group policy unless the employers put some money into the plan.) Financial institutions will often help the company determine which employees will participate in the plan, whether the employer will make contributions, and the goal in introducing this type of plan.

The Royal Bank's *The Definitive Guide to Managing Human Resources for Small Business Owners* offers some good advice on profit sharing. "The keys to a good profit-sharing plan are clarity of purpose and realistic performance standards. For example, many small businesses still pay a flat Christmas bonus to all employees at the end of the year, but it's not always clear in everyone's mind how it is linked to the company's profitability or whether individual performance had much impact.

"A profit-sharing format needs to be communicated to employees and linked to goals individuals have control over, such as their own productivity, sales volumes, or cost-saving initiatives."[2]

Karen Flavelle of Purdy's Chocolates has a workforce that is divided among factory, administration, and retail store personnel. She pays factory workers and store employees on an hourly basis. Management in the factory, office, and store are salaried. Full-time salaried employees are involved in a profit-sharing plan.

David Haslam of Presidential Plumbing Ltd. is considering putting in place a profit-sharing scheme in the future. He says, "Right now, what I do in lieu of a bonus is throw a fabulous Christmas party every year to give recognition to the employees. There are a lot of companies that don't do anything. In my industry, a bonus or profit-sharing atmosphere isn't commonplace, although I don't think it's a bad idea. It's an excellent way to motivate and stimulate your employees. Unfortunately, I haven't been in a financial position to offer that."

He goes on to say, "Our company is in the early stages, but actually one of my goals at some point in the future is to implement some sort of profit sharing, or work recognition. I think people would appreciate that."

2. Project Milestone and Completion Bonuses

Numerous companies, particularly those in the high-tech field, work on long-term projects. In order to reward and retain key employees, many of them are turning to such things as project completion bonuses, or bonuses related to the achievement of key project milestones. Project completion bonuses are different from profit-sharing bonuses because they are paid only when a project is finished. Long-term profit-sharing bonuses are based on the profits of the company as a whole and are generally paid out either at the end of the year or a defined longer-term period.

Project profit sharing is a method that groups employees whose talents match the needs of the project. A point system is set up based on the position of the employee, his or her use of professional development opportunities and his or her contribution to the project. If the project comes in under budget or prior to its deadline, a larger portion of the profits can be shared.

Full disclosure of the profit split is advised in this type of profit sharing. Its advantage over traditional profit sharing is that it provides a faster reward and positive reinforcement. However, companies using this method should be advised that there is a time commitment required to educate staff about it and provide them with other information on expenditures such as R & D. Constant communication is necessary in making the project profit-sharing system work.

In project work, profit sharing can be a worthwhile motivating tool. Participants in the Wisdom Exchange, a forum on business challenges co-sponsored by the Ontario government and a number of business service providers, noted that caution must be exercised so that project staff do not rush a job to reap the financial rewards, resulting in an unsatisfactory or returned product. One participating company stated that no profit sharing took place until the cheque came in from the client.

Project milestone or completion bonuses are not necessarily structured and announced as profit sharing, but in most cases they will inevitably be pegged in some manner to the success and profitability of the project.

Ellie Maggio of William M. Mercer Ltd. says that employers don't always wait for the project's completion to reward. "There are projects where sometimes, for certain positions, you can't wait a year or two to compensate or give some incentive. So, if a project's going to take 18 months, there may be some incentive payment for completing a significant milestone."

"Some employers," she says, "are actually giving people bonuses to stay around." Project milestones are being used in this way. It's not enough to have a bonus or incentive payment at the end of a project; as key milestones are met along the way, employers are recognizing the achievement with a bonus to keep employees focused and committed.

Project completion bonuses have become very important in order to ensure that a project is indeed completed. These bonuses are not only a way of saying thank-you but of also making it attractive for people to stay to the end of the project.

3. Special Awards

Periodic campaigns to increase sales and performance can pay off for employees in terms of both recognition and financial rewards. Campaigns also add excitement to the workplace and generate enthusiasm for projects. When goals are achieved or surpassed, a party can be held to honour employees and present awards.

S usan Niczowski of Summer Fresh Salads Inc. believes in incentive and bonus payments at various times for a variety of reasons. If the company's profitable, she says, she's more than willing to share with employees. But she also believes in other forms of recognition for employees whose extra efforts benefit the company.

"We received an award for our roasted red pepper dip, and everybody who worked on that particular product received a smaller version of the award. When we were named the forty-first company on PROFIT 100," Susan says, "we planned a big do to present each person in our organization with a mini-plaque saying thank you for putting us in the PROFIT 100."

In creative fields such as high-tech a sense of ownership in the company and even in the development of a new product or service can be a highly motivating and loyalty-producing factor. Wisdom Exchange participants recommended giving high-profile credit to critical performers. "Put their name on it" was one company's advice with regard to employees who develop successful products and services.

4. Employee Share Programs and Stock Options

One of the wealth-creating incentives employees and executives can receive from small and fast-growing companies is the option to purchase company shares or stock options. These plans give employees a chance to participate in the success of the business.

Shares and options can be granted to individuals in a number of ways:

- in lieu of compensation
- as a bonus based on performance
- by means of employees buying the shares at the independently set price

Shares

Most private companies hope that they will be successful enough to launch an initial public offering (IPO) and take the company public, so that its shares can be sold on a given stock exchange.

It is hoped that the publicly traded shares will have a higher value, thus allowing employees to sell their shares at a higher price than they paid for them.

Shares in a business are created at the time the company becomes incorporated. They can be expanded at any time in the future and may include different classes of shares. Some shares have voting rights, whereas others do not. Some pay dividends, and some do not. The value of the shares are set by independent outside audits and the share plan itself should be established with the help of a lawyer.

Stock Options

Stock options can be granted in the same way that shares are issued. Stock options are an arrangement by which an employee receives the "option," or right, to buy shares for a specified price during a specified time. Options are granted to an individual at the given price and can be exercised at any time during the agreed-upon term. For instance, the employee may wait until the company has gone public and the shares have risen before he or she chooses to buy the stocks in the option plan at the original set price. In this way the employee can make a substantial gain.

An example of this is a company in the computer industry. Because its profits had been increasing quite rapidly, it decided to give employees with good performance, stock options that would extend for a period of five years. These were given to the individual by the company at the initial price of $50 per share. The employees would then be able to keep the shares or cash them in at the end of the five years. Given the growth rate of the company, it is easy to predict that the $50 shares could well reach the value of $250 at the end of that period. So, clearly, this is a very attractive long-term way for employees to build up cash reserves.

If the company permits a long period from the date of the issue to the last date for exercising the option, this will encourage people to stay with the company and be fully committed to its success.

THE ADVANTAGES AND DISADVANTAGES OF SHARE AND STOCK OPTION SCHEMES

Advantages

- They increase the commitment of the employee to the company, since they own part of it.

- Employees are likely to become more cost- and profit-conscious.

- Additional money will be raised for the company as employees buy the shares.

- There is a potential for employees to increase their wealth as the company becomes more profitable and the value of the shares increases.

Disadvantages

- The value of the shares may not increase, since the company may not be as profitable as hoped: thus, these types of plans and bonuses are a gamble for the individual.

- Shares in a private company must be traded within the firm, which assumes that someone else wants to buy them.

- If shares and options are given out to too many people, the value of the stock can be diluted, making it less valuable than if it were held by only a few people.

Shares and options in high-tech companies are particularly attractive to younger people, who hope that they have joined the next Microsoft or Yahoo. Many will work for a company for a while to learn new skills, but if they see that it is not going to excel in the long term, they will move on to another company that offers shares and hope that that one becomes profitable.

The tax implications of shares and stock options need to be reviewed by an accountant. Basically, receipt by an employee of a stock option does not give rise to income when the option or share is issued. Tax only becomes payable when the option is disposed of, or exercised—i.e., when the shares are actually bought.

BENEFITS

This chapter will cover a broad range of benefits, such as dental and health, and it will discuss briefly the topic of pensions. It will then look at provisions for short-term disability as a way in which employees can insure themselves against being sick for up to six months. It will examine long-term disability where an employee is unable to work for very long periods of time, sometimes forever.

Benefits are being used increasingly as a way to attract and retain employees to companies. These are often in addition to the forms of compensation noted in the previous chapter. The provision of benefits is often used as an extra factor in attracting candidates to work for one organization over another that offers less attractive benefits.

Many employers consider that the cost of providing benefits accounts for 15 per cent of total compensation. Quite simply, this means that employers pay 15 per cent more to an individual than they would if they didn't offer benefits. However, they often find that the attraction and retention factor makes it well worth paying those extra costs.

In some cases, the costs of the benefits are shared by employers and employees. They may share the cost of the various plans equally, i.e., both parties split the cost fifty-fifty.

When small and growing companies offer benefit plans, they usually cover all employees because it would be unfair to discriminate between different types of employees. If a company decides it wishes to provide greater benefits to its more senior and long-term employees, it can do this by providing different and more costly benefit plans. As we'll discuss later, you can have benefit plans that provide basic coverage, or you can go for more deluxe packages with features that provide, for instance, more money in life insurance pay-outs.

Benefit considerations are important to people like me, who are used to having coverage with their previous organizations. I became aware of issues relating to benefits when I set up my own business five years ago. Up to that point health, dental, life insurance, and disability benefit coverage and premiums were provided through my employer. Deciding what coverage I needed was yet another aspect of creating my own business that required thought and added to the list of things that had to be done.

Once I made the decision on what type of benefits I required, I then had to think about how to get them. At that time, insurance companies and financial organizations did not pay as much attention to benefit coverage for small enterprises as they do today, particularly for companies with less than five employees. Through networking I was put in touch with a person who gives advice to the benefit plans of various professional and trade associations. He suggested that I join the Canadian Professional Sales Association (CPSA), which provides benefits for its members. I followed this advice and through the CPSA now have medical and dental benefits, disability insurance and life insurance, and am pleased with the services the organization offers.

David Haslam's company, Presidential Plumbing Ltd., offers a benefit package that covers 100 per cent of medical and 80 per cent of dental, and also provides some life and travel insurance coverage. David explains: "I wanted to do it to keep the men happy, and I wanted to attract others from a union environment. So, I wanted to compete on that level and it seems to have worked out quite well. Now we pay for half the benefits and the employee pays for the other half." He arranged for the coverage through a life insurance company, going through an insurance broker to put it into place.

COST OF BENEFIT PROGRAMS

As we mentioned, the cost of employee benefit insurance is estimated to be at least 15 per cent of total compensation costs, which is quite significant. As David Howe of Eckler Partners Ltd. says, "If you can get people to work for you with no benefits, it makes life a lot simpler, and a lot of younger people and part-time people would rather have the cash. If you say to them would you like the cash or would you like the benefits, what are they going to say?"

Typically the employer and the employee share in the cost of the benefit plans, with the employees making regular deductions from their wages and salaries on a weekly or monthly basis.

TYPES OF BENEFITS

Employee benefits include coverage for:

• Health and Dental Insurance
• Short-Term Disability
• Long-Term Disability
• Life Insurance

Health and Dental Insurance

Health and dental plans cover expenses such as the following:

• prescription drugs
• semi-private hospital
• paramedical practitioners such as chiropractors and physiotherapists
• routine dental expenses
• specialist dental care

Some companies have plans that even provide for eyeglasses. Others have a basic health plan, with no dental. Plans may be divided into the basic and the deluxe. Deluxe plans have more benefits but the insurance costs are higher. The type of plan that is put in place depends on the cost of insurance and the needs of the employee population.

Consider this example. A medium-size public relations company has a basic plan in which employees are covered for medical and hospital costs. However, they have no dental plan. Some employees asked that such a plan be included in the package because they wanted coverage for themselves and their families. Dental coverage can be very expensive, especially if the employees have young children with orthodontic needs. So a deluxe plan was put in place that covered dental work, and employees were asked to contribute half of the cost of the premiums for the extra plan. When you consider that this amounted to only about two or three dollars a month, it was well worth the small outlay.

Health and dental premiums are tax deductible. In the 1998 federal budget, measures were introduced to allow both incorporated and unincorporated business to deduct premiums for health and dental insurance. This health care is tax efficient because the employer gets a tax deduction on the premiums and the employees are not taxed when their expenses are reimbursed.

Short-Term Disability

Short-term disability covers any form of illness or accident whether it takes place at work or not. It is broader than the statutory workers' compensation that covers only accidents in the workplace.

People often look to companies to offer short-term disability plans that will cover their loss of salary and wages when they are sick for brief periods. Short-term disability (STD) generally refers to coverage periods of six months or less.

David Howe suggests that small business owners consider having STD coverage for their key people. However, he advises it may be less expensive to continue paying a sick employee's wages rather than to pay STD premiums.

The reason it is less expensive to continue paying a sick employee's wages, rather than paying the short-term disability premiums, is that these premiums are quite high. For instance, you may have to pay $5,000 a year in premiums, while for a lower-paid employee who's sick, it may be more economical to carry on paying their salary when you're only looking at $600 a week or so. Although you don't know how long the employee is going to be ill, paying their wages and salaries is often less than paying insurance premiums which, as noted, can be quite expensive.

Long-Term Disability

Long-term disability (LTD) benefits come into force after an individual has been unable to work for six months. It is very difficult for individuals to buy their own long-term disability insurance coverage. The reason for this is that insurance companies are reluctant to insure individuals because if they become ill, it may well cost the insurer a great deal of money. They frequently will not offer such insurance coverage because in return for perhaps $4,000 to 5,000 per annum in premiums, they can end up paying out a person's salary or wages for dozens of years—right up until that person is 65 years old. For them, clearly, this is not a very good insurance risk. Thus, the employer has to set up a plan with an insurance company or obtain these benefits through a professional or trade association.

David Howe notes, "Personally, I'd always have the employer pay the LTD premiums. When most people become disabled, the income they get is not large enough to pay much tax anyway. You're better off with the employer getting the tax deduction up front. Otherwise the employee has to pay the premiums out of after-tax income."

When an employee becomes disabled, they may get up to 80 per cent of their base income, not including bonuses or other forms of compensation. Although the benefits are taxable if the employer has paid the premiums, depending on the initial salary or wages of that person, it is unlikely the employee will have to pay much tax on their benefits, as the rate is usually low, say 20 per cent.

Thus, as David Howe points out, it is to the employer's advantage to pay the premiums and get any tax deduction up front. If the employee pays for the premiums, the benefits will not be taxable, but the premium must be paid from their after-tax income, and this can be quite a slice of money out of what may not be much to begin with.

Life Insurance

Life insurance needs to be considered from two angles. First, regarding the entrepreneur and any partners they might have when setting up a business, it is very important to have some life insurance coverage, both so the business will survive the loss of one partner, and so their families will have some income in the event of the early death of a partner or owner.

The other point to consider is that life insurance can be offered to some, if not all, the employees in the company.

Pensions

All employees, through payroll deductions, will contribute to the Canada Pension Plan or the Quebec equivalent. The premiums are determined by the government and pensions are paid out at the age of 65. At the time of writing, there are many discussions by actuaries and others that the CPP/QPP may not have enough money to allow people to retire and maintain an adequate standard of living. Thus, a number of individuals are anxious to invest as much money as possible in registered retirement plans.

The previous chapter discussed how companies can provide group registered retirement plans, which allow individuals to put up to 15 per cent of their earnings, tax-free, into an RRSP each year. A number of companies still have what are called defined contribution plans, where they will put money into a pension plan, rather than a benefits plan for an individual. But for the small business owner, this is just not a cost-effective proposition, which is why small businesses either provide no form of pension provision or contribute based on earnings and performance of the individual, into a group registered retirement plan for the individual.

Chapter 9, "Incentives," covers this topic much more thoroughly.

SOURCES OF BENEFITS
INSURANCE FOR SMALL BUSINESSES

There are a number of sources for small business owners to explore if they want to get benefit coverage for themselves and their employees. These are:

- insurance brokers (some specialize in small groups)
- insurance companies (the best known are Liberty Health and Blue Cross)
- banks and other financial institutions
- boards of trade/chambers of commerce
- professional and trade associations (e.g., those for professional engineers or chartered accountants, or bodies such as the Canadian Professional Sales Association, mentioned above.)

In order to find the best and most cost-effective insurance, it is useful to talk to any of the benefit providers noted above to find one that best suits your needs in terms of offering the kinds of benefits desired, and also, more importantly, that meets the needs of your pocketbook. By asking for details of insurance coverage from these different sources, you will certainly be able to come up with the kind of plan that is designed to meet your needs. Since many organizations are very anxious to get your business these days, it is possible to negotiate a cost-effective plan.

And don't forget networking. Asking other business owners how they handle the benefits question can be an invaluable source of suggestions and ideas as to the specific insurance, financial institution, or business group that can best help you design and obtain effective benefits.

Finally, it should be noted that establishing a benefits plan can be not only expensive but complex, and therefore it is just as easy to spend too much time as well as too much money on the process. For most companies the important thing will be to find a trustworthy source of assistance in designing an affordable plan conveniently.

David Howe of Eckler Partners comments, "Professional and trade associations won't necessarily be the cheapest place to look for benefit coverage. But what you really want to do is look for the easiest way, not the cheapest."

PAYROLL PROCESSES

This chapter looks at various payroll matters. It will cover the information of what is required to put a person on payroll and to get them paid. It will also deal with the various ways payroll can be processed.

REQUIREMENTS TO SET UP A PAYROLL

There are a number of things that an employer has to obtain from different government bodies in order to set up a business and to pay employees. These are noted below.

The Business Number

In order to start a new business the owner needs to get a business number from Revenue Canada. This will be the number under which any statutory deductions will be remitted to the government.

Employer's Health Tax

Employers are required to pay an Employer's Health Tax for every individual employee. It is necessary to apply to the government in the province where the business operates, for the rates and frequency of remitting the Employer's Health Tax. It should be noted that in Alberta and British Columbia health premiums are paid by the employee and not by the employer.

Workers' Compensation

The employer also has to find out the rates that they have to pay for workers' compensation. Workers' compensation has to be paid for every employee and this covers injuries incurred while at work. In Ontario this compensation is now the responsibility of the Workplace Safety Insurance Board, while the other provinces each have a Workers' Compensation Board. The rate that has to be paid for workers' compensation depends on the industry and is similar to an insurance premium. The more claims that are made on the board for employee injuries, the higher the premium that the individual company has to pay. A company will need to contact the appropriate workers' compensation organization for their province in order to find out what the rates are.

In determining the rate for an individual business, account is taken of whether the employer has any form of self-insurance for the organization, such as short-term disability (STD) or long-term disability (LTD) insurance. These plans cover injury and illness which are not incurred at work, whereas the workers' compensation insurance is strictly for injuries in the workplace. Having STD and LTD insurance plans reduces the workers' compensation rate that has to be paid for each employee.

Other Government Remittances

There are other forms of statutory deductions that have to be made from each individual's pay and sent to the federal government. These are for the Canada Pension Plan (CPP) and Employee Insurance (EI). In Quebec the QPP is paid to the Quebec government and is roughly equivalent to the CPP. Both CPP and EI are funded jointly by the employer and the employee. Rates are provided in the tables of deductions from Revenue Canada. These remittances, together with the federal and provincial income tax deductions, and the others noted above, need to be sent to the government. They are usually made on a monthly basis, but for larger payrolls, they can be done more frequently, say, weekly or biweekly.

INDIVIDUAL EMPLOYEE INFORMATION REQUIRED TO PROCESS PAYROLL

The following information is required in order to put a person on payroll:

• Legal Name

• Social Insurance Number

• Date of Birth

• Date of Hire

• Remuneration (whether it be in the form of wages, salaries, and bonuses, etc.)

• Employee's Address

• Mailing Address of Employee (if different from the above)

FREQUENCY OF PAYROLL

The organization has to determine how often it will pay people. This will depend on what best meets the needs of the business in relation to cash flow and the type of employees that are employed by that particular organization.

The most common payrolls are:

(a)   weekly (52 pay periods per year)
(b)   biweekly (26 pay periods per year)
(c)   semi-monthly (24 pay periods per year)
(d)   monthly (12 pay periods per year)

(a) Weekly: This type of payroll is suitable if the organization is small and has employees who do piecework. It may also suit organizations with high employee turnover or with contractors where periods of activities are varied. It may also meet the needs of employers who have a seasonal payroll where they employ many people at one given time of year.

(b) Biweekly: This is the most common pay cycle for employers. Employees are paid on the same day every two weeks, i.e., every second Friday. It is much easier to administer and process for groups of almost any size and is appropriate for all pay situations. It is useful in that it accommodates both hourly and salaried employees and meets all the statutory requirements for each province.

(c) Semi-Monthly: This payroll is done only twice a month, usually on the fifteenth day and the last day of each month. This is most appropriate for large groups because there is more time for payroll processing and it is easier for accounting purposes since it requires only 24 pay periods instead of 26. This type of semi-monthly pay meets all the statutory requirements for all provinces except Quebec. There, Quebec provincial law requires all employees be paid every 14 days, thus making the biweekly pay period mandatory. However, in certain circumstances Quebec may allow a semi-monthly payroll.

(d) Monthly: Monthly payroll is relatively rare in Canada and when used, is often reserved for more senior employees in a company. It can also be used when more complicated payrolls are involved.

PROCESSING OF PAYROLL

There are two choices for processing payroll. It can be done in-house by a CFO or a payroll person, or by a third-party processor, such as a bank or a payroll organization.

In-House Payroll

If a smaller organization—less than four employees—chooses to do its payroll processing itself, it usually uses a bookkeeping/accounting process. The process is completed either by using a manual balance sheet with running totals for statutory deductions, or by means of an electronic tax table called WINTOD which is available from any Revenue Canada office. Statutory deductions are calculated using the paper table of deductions from the government or WINTOD. It is the responsibility of the employer to remit all statutory deductions to the appropriate federal and provincial bodies.

ADVANTAGES AND DISADVANTAGES OF IN-HOUSE PAYROLL

Advantages

- Little or no cost is incurred, other than the time of the person processing the payroll
- It is simple, cost-effective, and relatively easy to maintain

Disadvantages

- Under this method there is a greater degree of room for error since calculations are done manually.

- Transposition errors and the lack of an actual register total other than a spreadsheet or bookkeeping process may make it difficult to reconcile all figures and provide a reconcilable year-end payroll report.

- Year-end tax documents and Records of Employment required when an employee leaves the company may be incorrect when they are given either to the individual or to the government, since they are produced manually.

- Payroll processing and reporting can be time-consuming if the payroll is complicated or gets larger.

On balance in-house processing is an effective method of doing a payroll for a small group of employees but does not allow for direct deposit of pay to an employee bank account. Pay cheques must be cut and this, of course, carries the risk of their being lost or stolen.

Larger organizations that do in-house processing can do direct deposits to employee bank accounts if they use payroll software such as PeopleSoft, which will send deposits to the bank for posting.

Third-Party Payroll Processing

Third-party payroll processing is done by a bank or other major payroll provider. Such institutions include all the major banks and private payroll operators such as ADP and Ceredian. A third-party processor offers a wide degree of support to the individual and the costs will vary according to the services required.

They will give the employer software or manual processes to complete relating to the details of pay and any changes throughout the pay period. The third-party provider simply processes the information provided, but the actual data is always entered by the employer. If errors do occur in data input it is the responsibility of the business to correct these errors.

ADVANTAGES AND DISADVANTAGES OF THIRD-PARTY PAYROLL PROCESSING

Advantages

- The third-party processor will remit statutory deductions as requested and pay them directly to the appropriate government organization. The business is charged according to the number of pay periods and customized reports required by the business.

- This option allows for direct deposit of pay cheques to an employee account if required.

- Technical support is often offered by these organizations through a call centre. Banks and other organizations may provide a relationship manager or client manager that can be the first line of contact to the organization should a problem arise.

- The third-party provider has the ability to produce year-end documents such as T4s, which are required for individuals to complete their income tax returns. They will also provide Records of Employment which are necessary when an employee leaves the organization.

Disadvantages

- There is a cost incurred in using a third-party processor, which depends on the number of payrolls required and the number of employees for whom this payroll is being processed.

Even very small organizations often ask banks or payroll processors to do the payroll for them because it takes away the time that is better spent in marketing and selling or on producing goods and services required by customers. However, if money is tight many employers choose to do the payroll themselves.

DEVELOPMENT

With smaller businesses, employees are able to walk into the president's office and talk with her.

—Lynda Bowles, Deloitte and Touche

Quality employees often choose a small business in hopes of finding a more creative and less conventional workplace. Keeping them happy and productive becomes one of the key human resources challenges for the busy entrepreneur lucky enough to attract them. In this section, we will examine some of the things an effective manager can do to keep employees involved and committed to the company's goals.

We start with Chapter 12, "Good Communications and New Employee Orientation," which covers orienting the new employee to the company and keeping the lines of communications open.

In Chapter 13, "Performance Reviews," the performance review process looks at formal reviews between the company and the individual, which form the basis of paying out bonuses, individual development plans, and setting expectations for the next year.

Chapter 14, "Training and Development," looks at issues such as whether to have experienced people or train greenhorns, as well as how to go about that training.

Chapter 15, "Problem Employees: Performance Improvement," looks at how to deal with problem employees and the use of the performance improvement process.

Chapter 16, "Termination Procedures," tells how to fire employees and looks at employee termination, both voluntary and involuntary.

CHAPTER TWELVE

GOOD COMMUNICATIONS AND NEW EMPLOYEE ORIENTATION

Over my many years as a human resources professional, I have come to believe that the best of HR practice comes down to just one word: communications. This is as true for small and medium-size businesses as it is for immense corporations; in fact, the entrepreneur has an important advantage over his or her larger competitors in this area. Lynda Bowles of Deloitte and Touche explains: "In the larger firm you may feel you're making a contribution, and although it's important, you have difficulty seeing the effects of your contribution. In construction or on the line at GM, each person wonders what difference it makes whether they tighten that screw or not? It makes a hell of a difference, but they just can't see that. With smaller businesses the importance of each person is often more evident."

The entrepreneurs I interviewed sounded the same theme: one valuable asset they have is their ability to share the excitement of a growing business with their employees. Without this sharing, more than one warned, the talented people who are attracted to small business will lose hope of seeing their efforts acknowledged and will leave. David Anderson of CANATOM NPM told me, "My approach is the opposite to some people's and some companies', where information is restricted at various levels and doesn't flow down. I think that devalues your employees. I let financial information go down in the company. I don't think it hurts for the employees to know how we're doing." Without this free flow of information, he went on, "you don't get as much as your employees can give, and in the end they get disenchanted and leave."

If what David says is true, then small business operators must treat good communications as good business, not just good philosophy. Look at it this way. Good communications on the job is above all pragmatic: it begins with making certain that everyone on staff understands the products and/or services the company sells. It also identifies a technique entrepreneurs can use to share their powerful vision of business growth with their employees.

But the logic of good communications can carry the creative entrepreneur much farther. For example, small business operators, especially in the high-tech industries, worry about losing their best employees to higher-paying competitors.

Lynda Bowles points out an approach with real potential: "The needs of individuals are changing. Employees need flexibility in their work to meet the other demands/challenges of their lives They no longer live to work. They work to live. When evaluating a job, they may be willing to take less of income to have a more balanced life. They value their time much more than my generation. I know there are people at the office who say, I don't work on Monday nights. I'm doing something, or I've got another commitment. They may be willing to work at different times—not the normal nine to five routine. I think you have to respect their needs, keeping the company's long-term goals in mind."

Open communications, with the goal of making work mutually beneficial to both company and employee at all times, could help the entrepreneur convince promising young people they can have both a career with the company and still have a fulfilling life outside work.

The discussion that follows focuses on two important opportunities for good communications: new employee orientation and staff meetings.

GOOD COMMUNICATIONS
STARTS AT EMPLOYEE ORIENTATION

Small business operators should give as much attention to the orientation of new employees as they give to recruitment; in fact, good orientation depends very much on the same principles that were discussed above in Part Two, "The Recruiting Process." Just as the recruitment interview should be treated as a public relations exercise, so too should orientation. There should be the same attention to presentation quality, the same clarity of information, and the same strength of documentation.

First, orientation should be conducted in a professional manner. Consider using videos and quizzes to get people involved. Try to conduct orientation for several employees at one time: this not only saves time but also starts the process of building relationships among the employees. The customary tour of the facilities should be thorough and practical: Where are the washrooms? How do you get a cup of coffee? How do the phones work?

For some aspects of orientation, such as brief meetings with all key personnel with whom a new employee will be working closely, a group approach is not appropriate. The small business operator should emphasize to all staff that the job of orientation is everyone's responsibility and can go on for weeks after the new employee's first day.

Second, orientation should provide clear, helpful information about the company. A group orientation should include a brief presentation by a senior manager, in which such topics as the following are discussed:

- company history
- mission statement
- basics of company structure
- guidelines on HR procedures
- updating of current business strategy
- current product lines and services

New employees should have time to ask questions and introduce themselves to the manager making the presentation.

Third, an employee should receive some material to take away, if only directions on how to make claims through benefit plans, such as the insurance provisions. But it could be more. Even a small company should have a mission statement, an organizational chart, a telephone list, emergency numbers, and so on. A folder with this information printed out could make a very effective starting kit to present to each new employee. Whatever you provide, it should impress the employee with its practicality and its professional quality. As anyone knows who has attempted to use a typical software manual, it isn't a question of quantity. It's a question of efficiency.

> Kieran O'Briain of Kee Transport paints a vivid picture of some of the bright spots and some of the problems of orientation as it is done at Kee Transport.
>
> "One of the areas that I have taken an interest in is that initial orientation. That first conversation is not happening in the way it should. Right now, the orientation tends to concentrate on money—you know, hand in your paperwork and do this and this and this. That is all fine—it's got to be done—but underlying that you have to build the teamwork—the team philosophy, the family philosophy—somehow that has to soak in."

GOOD COMMUNICATIONS ON THE JOB: STAFF MEETINGS

Management needs to deliver on the promise that it will always be accessible to employees and that employees will be able to have a high degree of involvement in the running of their department or the company. If this was promised in the orientation and job offer stages, then management must make sure that this indeed does happen.

The Dilbert cartoons provide wonderful examples of how meetings are used to:

• waste time

• have free coffee and doughnuts

• generally chat about everything except work

Make sure your company's meetings do not become associated with these kinds of activities. Meetings are a very important form of sharing information and getting decisions made. If not used correctly, they can be a tremendous waste of time, money, and productivity as people sitting in meetings are not performing the duties that they're being paid to do and may not be meeting their various customer needs.

Good communications should mean that the busy entrepreneur makes himself or herself available to employees, demonstrating to them that their suggestions and ideas matter. This interaction should be one-on-one. Remember what Lynda Bowles says about the door of the small business president being open to all employees. Managers must make themselves available to employees through company meetings.

Managers have to set up regular meetings that provide employees with secure opportunities for making practical suggestions, airing complaints, and resolving potentially disruptive conflicts. Such meetings are living proof to employees that teamwork is more than just a slogan. The sense of importance that comes from being involved should translate into increased productivity as well as good employee and customer relations.

Managers have to bring something else to those meetings. Each manager is the custodian of the big picture of the company and must make that overall corporate vision a living part of each employee's understanding of the job. Every discussion of recent performance should include a perspective provided by the manager that places events in the context of the company's business plan and growth strategy.

SOME TIPS ON GOOD COMMUNICATING

Managers can keep the lines of communications open with employees:

- Encourage employees to promote each other's skills; every company member should be "talking proud" about the company and about each other.
- Empower employees to make decisions within their area of responsibility, e.g., closing sales.
- Be responsive to employee feedback on how to improve operations.
- Involve staff in decision making with regard to changes affecting them.
- Counsel employees on ways to improve performance.
- Do not overreact to mistakes, especially first-time cases.

The Characteristics of a Good Meeting

A general principle applicable to all meetings is that they should be conducted in a professional, expeditious manner. Meetings are work, not recreation, and the discipline of the workplace should apply to them.

A second important guideline is that the meeting should be as inclusive as possible. One company has had excellent results with involving both office and plant staff equally in consultation. Feedback to the CEO has been excellent. Advantages include:

- Important information about company strategy is widely available and is incorporated into all details of production.

- Insights into customers, particularly changes in customers' culture, are shared.

- Broader input from employees permits more informed decision making.

TIPS FOR GOOD MEETINGS

- Hold regular general meetings (e.g., every two weeks) that feature substantive updates on events since the last meeting. Encourage questions, and answer them fully. If an employee objects to an answer, come back once, then move the discussion on.

- The general meetings should not only answer employees' questions, but should give information about the company—where it's going, any issues facing it—and encourage solutions and the development of action plans.

- Avoid luncheon meetings. They do not generate good employee involvement. People are usually more interested in getting out to eat and may resent the fact that they're having to work through their lunch hour. It's far better to have meetings first thing in the morning or last thing in the afternoon when, hopefully, you will get much better attention from people.

- Set strict time limits for meetings in which decisions must be made. Avoid lengthy meetings, particularly when work is being held up pending the meeting's outcome. Do set strict time limits and keep meetings as short as possible. This keeps people's attention and it makes them focus on the task at hand. It also stops the urge that we all have sometimes to just generally chat. Have an agenda printed and distributed.

- Another effective method is to have a one-hour management meeting once a month that focuses on assigning projects to subgroups who then work together and report back at the next meeting. Such management meetings can provide an excellent reality check: Are staff members in alignment with the company philosophy?

CHAPTER THIRTEEN

PERFORMANCE REVIEWS

Review of performance is an ongoing process, but managers should also schedule a formal process of review—either at the end of the year, the end of a project, or some other interval—to examine an individual's performance in relation to the expectations that were set at the beginning of the performance period. This formal process, called a performance review, has several benefits. First, it provides a context for manager and employee to confirm that they have a common understanding of the company's business plans and priorities and to assess the employee's recent performance in relation to the overall company program.

It helps manager and employee to identify any problems that have hindered the achievement of performance objectives and encourages them to look together for solutions. For instance, an individual may not have been able to achieve a particular objective because promised training was not provided, the employee was not kept informed about changing objectives, or technology was not upgraded. The formal performance review also replaces vague appraisals such as, "You've done a really great job and here's a bonus," with a direct link between compensation and an employee's contributions to company productivity during a performance period. Thus, a performance review is particularly important if, as described in Chapter 9, incentives are linked to an employee's achievement of performance objectives.

Finally, a performance review is useful for setting goals for the coming year, which is important both for guiding individual achievement and for realizing business goals and objectives.

Performance appraisals are as vital to the operator of a small or medium-size business as they are for large corporations, and yet, according to Lynda Bowles of Deloitte and Touche, they are too often omitted by the busy entrepreneur. It may be time pressure or a lack of familiarity with particular skills of people management, Lynda says, but an employee needs "that positive reinforcement" that a formal performance review process can give.

There are a variety of reasons why performance reviews are not done. These generally fall into the category of the employer claiming they don't have enough time to do them. Indeed, the time for preparation and sitting down with employees does take a fair bit of time if done correctly.

Secondly, employers often don't want to confront employees with difficult issues. They don't like telling them that they haven't met their goals. They don't like telling them that they need to improve in certain areas. So, generally, employers tend to avoid performance reviews.

The final point is that performance reviews can be stressful. For whatever reason, having discussions about past performance creates stress for both the individual employee and for the manager and entrepreneur/business owner.

PREPARING FOR THE REVIEW

Both management and employees should prepare thoroughly for the meeting. Just as with other formal meetings discussed in previous chapters, managers must provide leadership to the company by treating the performance review as an integral part of operations. They must set a standard by their own level of preparation and by allowing time for the employee to get ready as well. Sufficient time should be set aside for conducting the review itself, and the meeting should take place in a room that is free from potential distraction such as telephones or computers. Frequent interruptions not only disrupt communications, but they often leave the employee feeling unappreciated and uncertain about what is expected for future performance.

Reviewer Preparation

Reviewers should come to the meeting prepared to talk both about the performance period just completed and the one about to start.

REVIEWER PREPARATION FOR PERFORMANCE REVIEW

For an effective review of the past, the reviewer should:

- Verify the goals and objectives set for the individual at the beginning of the review period, using either the previous year's performance review or the employee's job description. These goals and objectives should have been set jointly between the individual and his or her manager and should be realistic in terms of what has been required of the employee for the past year. It goes without saying that these goals and objectives should have been achievable as well as realistic.

- Gather data from as many sources as possible, including input from the employee's colleagues and co-workers, to develop a thorough, balanced assessment of recent performance. To avoid gossip and to get really good feedback from employees, it's important to gather data by asking some very specific questions:

  – What did the employee achieve?
  – How good was he or she as a co-worker?
  – What would you say was his or her major strengths were?
  – Were there any opportunities for improvement?

  By keeping this on a very businesslike, professional basis, you should avoid any gossip or putting down of the individual when the data is collected.

- Document achievements and areas in which improvement is needed. Throughout the course of the year, or during the review period, the manager needs to note in writing the areas in which the employee did particularly well. This means keeping copies of reports as examples, as well as notes and specific examples of things in areas in which the employee did particularly well. It may also mean keeping notes of where there is need for improvement—for instance, achievement of results, timekeeping, etc. It is essential to keep a file on the individual throughout the year that can be used as the basis for the performance discussions. It's very easy to forget things, both good and bad, that have happened over the course of a year or during the review period.

- List objectives for the upcoming performance period, including both productivity goals and objectives in skill enhancement. It is important that the manager doing the review list the objectives that are required of the employee for the coming period, or the business goals that have to be achieved. This then leads to the stage in which the individual and the manager need to agree and have a discussion in terms of what objectives can be achieved and what is feasible throughout the coming year.

Employee Preparation

The individual being reviewed also needs to prepare. The checklist below suggests some areas employees should be encouraged to consider before coming to the meeting.

EMPLOYEE PREPARATION FOR PERFORMANCE REVIEW

- What did you achieve during the performance period?
- Did you meet the objectives set for the period?
- If you fell short, what obstacles prevented you from achieving your goals and objectives?
- What can your supervisor or manager do to help improve your performance?
- What training and development do you need, and do you know where you can get it?
- Do you want to stay in your current position? How would you like to see your job change?
- What are your goals for the future? What path of advancement within the company would you like to follow?

THE PERFORMANCE REVIEW MEETING

The performance review is one of the key occasions in the company year that provides for communications between management and employees. The small business operator should look on this as an opportunity to build the team atmosphere, which is so essential, according to entrepreneurs and HR professionals alike, to the success of a growing company. There are several ways to improve communications at the meeting and to make it a basis for future effective communications.

The manager should discuss both achievements and areas needing improvement. Don't be wholly negative but, on the other hand, don't gloss over problem areas. Be specific. Avoid phrases such as "usually" or "always" in favour of thoroughly documented examples.

It is important that the manager discuss problem areas—what happened and how it happened—being very specific and asking the employee for his or her own ideas for improvement. Again, it is equally important to make sure that the employee doesn't give excuses but takes responsibility for improvement. Also, be specific in setting objectives for the coming year: set timetables, and quantify levels of increased productivity as a percentage improvement over current performance. It is important to be extremely clear about what the objectives are and state in numerically specific terms what is required—the number of sales, the number of reports to be prepared, the number of customers to be served, the number of units to be manufactured. Be very, very specific, and give timetables as well as the improvements required. The more specific you can be, the better off everyone is.

If the manager and employee agree that improvement is needed in a particular area, the program for development should be thoroughly defined. A specific training program, and a time allotment for it, should be set. Furthermore, the focus should be on demonstrating that the employee has gained the necessary job competency, not simply that he or she attended a particular course.

At the end of the review, make sure that everything is documented and put in the employee's file. This documentation will serve as a basis for the next performance review and also provide a clear and documented guide for the pay-out of any performance bonuses that have been agreed to.

Once all points are documented and put in the employee file, the agreement, which is indeed what it is, should be signed by both the employee and the manager. Everything about a performance review should be done in a collaborative fashion. If someone simply tells someone else what to do, it is unlikely that there will be commitment to getting things done.

With good communications as the starting point, the reviewer and employee should work to accomplish three tasks in the meeting:

1. Review Performance during the Review Period—whether it is a particular project, the previous quarter, or the past year—and discuss compensation for that performance.

2. Set Objectives and Goals for the Next Period—whether it be a defined time span or a specific project—and include the required measurement steps for those objectives and goals.

3. Assess the Development Needs of Individuals in relation to performance and to make development plans to meet those needs.

1. Review Performance during the Review Period

The manager and the employee first need to verify that they agree on the goals and results that were expected over the defined period. If there was no review or goal setting over the past review period, the reviewer and the employee need to agree on what expectations were implied. In the absence of specific goals for a time period, the original job description may be useful in characterizing objectives for a position.

If the employee and the manager disagree on performance over the past review period, I would suggest you proceed as follows.

The area of discussion needs to be covered thoroughly, and if there is no agreement, it should be noted on the performance appraisal document. The manager will outline what he or she thought the performance was, and the employee can then give an explanatory note as to why they disagree. This is the fairest way of doing things and shows that there was some cause for concern. The important thing then is to discuss what needs to be done and to set goals for the next year to ensure that the areas that did not achieve required results are brought up to standard during the following period.

Next, the reviewer and the employee need to agree on what was achieved and how well it was achieved. It may be useful to display on a scale of one to five (one being low and five high) the range of expectations that were set and then use the scale to discuss the manager's assessment and the employee's response. Such a scale can be particularly important in determining whether or not an individual is eligible to receive a performance bonus previously agreed upon. For instance, if $10,000 was to be given after full achievement of all objectives, but objectives were not met, a decision has to be made as to how much of the bonus, if any, is going to be paid. For example, if half of the objectives were met, does the employee get $5,000?

The review should assess performance in terms of both particular productivity targets and employee advancement in core competencies. As indicated in Chapter 4, "Job Descriptions and Competency Profiles," HR theory and practice demonstrate that it is valuable to reward employees not only for specific tasks, but also for advancement in the skills and knowledge recognized as crucial to good job performance—that is, in their achievement of the core competencies of their position. Thus, a performance review should consider the extent to which an employee demonstrated that he or she possesses technical and general competencies. For instance, if at the previous review it was decided that the employee needed to develop knowledge of a particular computer program or application, the review should consider whether that new knowledge has been demonstrated by the employee. It is important to emphasize that it is not just about taking the course; being able to put the new knowledge to work is essential.

2. Set Objectives and Goals for the Next Period

The second part of the performance review process is setting goals and objectives for the future, and setting them together is important to both manager and employee. The setting of goals for the next period can take place in the same review meeting or can be done in a separate one. A full review of the past year's performance, of next year's performance, and setting development plans can take up to two hours if done properly. Some people like to do the whole thing in one meeting. Others prefer to separate the review of the past year's performance and the setting of goals and objectives and development plans into two meetings. It all depends on what meets the needs of the individual and, of course, time commitments and people's availability. Goals:

- formalize what has to be accomplished
- identify who is responsible for reaching the set goal
- give a timetable for completing a project
- focus on the costs that will be incurred in achieving the set goal

Managers and employees should work together to set the employee's objectives for the next work period. Five to six goals should be identified; do not try to list any more than that because of the danger of dissipating energy over too many projects.

The first step in formulating a goal is to identify an area for improvement such as:

- developing new business in a particular area
- developing a new computer software application
- improving current customer relationships
- improving office procedures
- bringing in a specified number of new clients or new sales

SMART GOALS

For each goal, specific objectives and measures should be set. These need to be SMART[1]:

S **Specific**   Be very clear in terms of what is required (for example, 500 sales, or new customers signed up within the year).

M **Measurable**   The measurable part would be a specific number such as 500 customers.

A **Action-Oriented**   Determine how you're going to get those customers, and set action plans to do that.

R **Realistic**   Would getting 500 customers be realistic? If not, perhaps the number should be reduced to 300. If it's far too easy, perhaps it should be increased to 700.

T **Time- and Resource-Constrained**   Set a specific time period, such as within the coming year.

For example, for the project of bringing in new sales, the specific objective might be to bring in five new sales within the next ten weeks.

Finally, the manager and employee should draw up an action plan for reaching the goal: who will work on the project with the employee, what particular techniques should be tried to achieve the goal, what consultation will be needed to make interim adjustments during the period. For example, the employee may attend upcoming trade shows or schedule a trip into a new market area to follow up leads on new clients.

A KEY GOAL SHOULD TAKE THE FOLLOWING FORM:

The employee will bring in five new sales within the next ten weeks both by maintaining regular sales contacts and by attending two upcoming trade shows. While the employee is preparing for and attending those shows, the manager will provide maintenance for existing accounts on the employee's behalf.

3. Assess the Development Needs of Individuals

The third part of the review process consists of looking at the individual's development needs. The course of development should take into account both shortcomings identified from the review of the previous period and the skills and knowledge requirements to meet the key goals set for the new period. The manager and employee working together should agree on the employee's current level of skills and knowledge, define the new levels towards which the employee should be working, and determine how the gap between the two is to be filled.

The assessment of the needs of the individual should define both the new requirements for the individual and how they're going to achieve them. For instance, is this going to be done through on-the-job training, external courses, or mentoring and coaching from other employees. This is covered much more thoroughly in the next chapter, "Training and Development."

It is essential to be specific. For instance, are these skills and knowledge requirements—that is, competencies—going to be developed by:

- coaching from the person doing the review?
- coaching from a manager in a different area of the business?
- coaching from peers?
- membership in outside associations that provide particular knowledge?
- attending internal or external training programs?
- working on assignments in other parts of the business?

It is not enough for the individual to say that she or he will attend such-and-such a course. Note the name of the course, when the employee will take it, and what other things he or she is going to do to learn a particular competency. Remember that the focus is on demonstrating the competency and making it a part of the everyday working life.

Employee development is important, especially in the high-tech and computer technology industries. People who join high-tech companies are looking for training to keep their skills current in a rapidly changing market. To retain good employees, managers must demonstrate their commitment to training and incorporate discussions of training into performance reviews.

In some cases, provision of training and development is as important as that of salaries, bonuses, and wages. Particularly in high-tech areas, keeping up to date with new skills and applications is the only way that an employee can remain employable. Individuals are often prepared to join a new company just to learn a particular skill, and they find that this is much more important than having a high compensation package.

TRAINING AND DEVELOPMENT

Training and development are important for all businesses and are particularly critical for small organizations. Experienced, competent people contribute to both the productivity and profitability of the company. Remaining competitive depends in large measure on ensuring that your workforce is trained and up to date with ever-changing skills and knowledge, especially in today's global economy, in which keeping up with new methods is so important. Despite the clear need to keep employees current, small organizations often show a reluctance to train. This can be due to cost or the desire not to have people away from their job for any length of time.

While training and development can be expensive—anywhere from $200 to $1,000 per day—it is still considered worthwhile in terms of achieving the long-term benefits of the company and the individual. Training expenses accrue not only from the actual cost of providing on- or off-the-job training, but also from loss of productivity while employees are away being trained. Nonetheless, it is still necessary to provide this training;

otherwise, companies discover how easy it is to fall behind both in terms of competence and meeting customers' needs.

There is another component to this reluctance, however. Many companies fear that if their employees are too well trained, they will move to another employer that pays more or offers other opportunities. In order to overcome this, some companies will train an employee so that he or she can be promoted to the next level within the organization and will want to stay with it.

This chapter will consider the basic issues relating to training and development. It will look at the advantages of hiring experienced people versus training inexperienced ones, the need for organizational and individual development, and the different approaches to training and development.

HIRING EXPERIENCE OR TRAINING

Are small businesses better off hiring experienced people or inexperienced ones who can train themselves? The sample of small business owners that I interviewed hired predominantly experienced people. Experienced people are preferred for three reasons:

1. They can be productive immediately because they have the required experience.

2. They add to the skills of the existing management team as well as the other employees.

3. They are less costly to the organization because training and development can be expensive.

As Lynda Bowles of Deloitte and Touche notes, "If you can hire a trained individual, usually at someone else's expense, you are better off."

Susan Niczowski of Summer Fresh Salads Inc. knows that it is not only expensive but time-consuming to train inexperienced people in a specialized field. "For somebody to get to know the ins and outs of our particular organization," she says, "would take a good six to nine months, because we have a large array of products. People with three to five years' experience really feel free in our organization within a month or so, while those who are totally green, just out of school, take a good year to understand it."

Susan says that in the beginning, Summer Fresh Salads Inc. had time to train people right out of school, but as the company grew, there was no longer time or energy available to train new employees in the ways of the business. "Now we're hiring more and more trained people," she says, "and we're at the point right now where we need people with more advanced training as well."

Karen Flavelle of Purdy's Chocolates says that her company does a lot of training of casual hires in the factory or part-timers in their stores, "but we wouldn't really train managers. We mostly hire people with experience. They would come in with some experience and then we'd help them grow into what we might need for the future."

David Anderson of CANATOM NPM definitely wants to hire experienced people: "I'm of the view that the obligation of my company these days is to provide people with an interesting job and an interesting place to work. If they come and work for me for six weeks, six months, or six years, they will become a better, more valuable commodity in the market place because of that experience. I'm not going to train them to do what I want them to do."

Thus, in the dilemma over whether to hire trained or untrained people, successful small businesses go both ways, but there is a distinct leaning to the trained and experienced worker. They hire trained people for managerial and highly skilled positions, and allow room for hiring young and untrained workers in entry-level positions, although even there they often prefer already trained people.

In *Secrets of Success from Canada's Fastest-Growing Companies*, Rick Spence states that, "While many PROFIT 100 entrepreneurs are happy hiring young and inexperienced people for production or entry-level positions, they take a different approach to filling their management needs. As their companies grow they know they need higher and higher levels of skills in operations, finance, marketing, and sales. Particularly tested is a young company's commitment to promoting from within. But the smartest and most far-sighted of PROFIT 100 entrepreneurs understand that the future of the company cannot be entrusted to amateurs, so they do their best to recruit high quality, professional help."[1]

Hiring Greenhorns

Some companies prefer to hire a mixture of experienced and less-experienced people. The reasoning behind this thinking is that greenhorns:

• are less expensive to hire

• can be trained in the particular techniques and style of the company

• can to be trained to the standards already in place

For David Haslam, whose company, Presidential Plumbing Ltd., does on-site construction jobs, experience is essential to the successful completion of projects, but hiring only experience is expensive. Further, there is the advantage in hiring apprentices that you get to train them to your own standards. "We do a mixture of both," David says. "We hire fully licensed plumbers, but we also hire apprentices and people with absolutely no experience in the construction industry, and we train them from the ground up. We put them with licensed plumbers and then we register them with the school that the government provides. We put them through a five-year program to have them become a full-fledged licensed plumber.

"Right now I have four apprentices working for me," he continues, "and out of those four, two had no experience. Others have been put through the apprenticeship program and they're licensed plumbers at this point." David likes the option of hiring a combination of licensed plumbers and apprentices that he can train because "we have a different way of doing business. We want to make sure that things are done right and we want them done our way."

David Marshall of Ergonomic Accessories Inc., which supplies ergonomically designed furniture, has hired people to work in his company from the insurance, pharmaceutical, and telecommunications industries. He then trains them in "The Ergonomic Way." David also has a professional kinesiologist on staff who initially had no sales background but who was trained in sales techniques by his colleagues; this proved to be very effective. In this manner, the various specialists in the company provide one-on-one training for each other.

TRAINING AS AN ATTRACTION AND RETENTION TOOL

If only it were as simple as hiring trained, experienced people whenever you can, and training only the new, inexperienced employees who come your way. The fact is that trained, experienced people still require and demand ongoing training. Many of them will not look at a company unless it includes training and education as a basic component of its culture and its employment offer. The provision of ongoing training and development is often a decisive feature in attracting and retaining many of today's employees.

Many knowledge workers in the high-tech area will only join organizations in which they know they will be trained in the latest software applications or work in a highly developed and up-to-date technical environment. Others will only join a company that has a good reputation in its field because they know that they will learn specific skills and knowledge from the people in that company. In this way, knowledge workers ensure their employability in both the current organization and any others they might be interested in joining in the future. Keeping up to date often provides a guarantee of employability, so it is no surprise that the provision of training and development is such a key component in attracting people.

And there are many fields besides high-tech that require knowledge workers. The same principle always applies, particularly whenever a certain skill or function is in demand: good workers or job candidates are likely to look elsewhere if your company does not help them keep up with their field or advance to new skills.

Thus, many entrepreneurs and small business owners take on the task of training people. As Rick Spence stated, "Enlightened entrepreneurs have found that the proper training program can not only boost employee skills but also acts as a prized benefit or incentive. For some employees training is the route to new skills, a better job, and more money. But to many others, especially where training funds are used not so much for on-the-job skills training but for a variety of educational purposes, it's a sign that the company cares and is willing to invest money in their future."

Spence also stated: "A 1994 StatsCan study of 1,480 growth firms found that 53 per cent offered their employees training. The PROFIT 100 survey, which represents the veritable tip of the iceberg when it comes to growth companies, found an even greater commitment: 81 of Canada's 100 Fastest-Growing Companies invest in employee training. In fact, the amount they spend on training has grown consistently over the six years that PROFIT has researched that statistic, to the point where PROFIT 100 companies now spend a full 1.8 per cent of revenues upgrading the skills of their employees."[2]

Ongoing Training and Development

As soon as a person is hired into the firm, there is a need to begin training. Rapid changes in technology, products, and business applications make it necessary for small firms to devote time to the ongoing training and development of their staff. In other words, your company most likely will need employees whose skills are constantly upgraded because it will constantly have to adapt to new conditions and methods in order to meet new competitive challenges. Training is not only necessary to keep the skill of the creative person current; it also contributes to your company's needs and goals.

Thus, training and development can be considered from two angles: the organization and the employee.

1. Organizational Requirements: What skills and knowledge does your organization require to keep it up to date and competitive?

2. Individual Training and Development Requirements: What are the skills and knowledge that the individual employee requires to develop and perform the job at the highest possible level?

Organizational Requirements

When thinking about their organizations' training and development needs, small business entrepreneurs should consider how they can stay on the leading edge of the skills and knowledge required by their customers and by the business environment in general. It is even better if they can think ahead and be prepared for the ever-changing demands of the market place in the next few years.

This means getting back to the fundamental business plan in which you identified where you want to be and how you are positioning your company within the business areas in which you plan to excel. The next step is to define the skills required to meet current business needs and those required to achieve your future business plans.

Mabel Jakimtschuk, who owns and operates Sherwood Village Spa, believes strongly in ongoing training for her employees. In the business of skincare and aesthetics, product knowledge and client services constantly need updating in order to compete against similar businesses. Although she prefers to hire experienced people, she provides ongoing training within her company and by means of mentoring. She is also a firm believer in specific education. Her employees do this educational broadening and upgrading of their skills after work hours. Sherwood Village Spa finds out about the programs and distributes the information to employees, encourages them to take courses, and pays the full tuition and costs when they enrol in one of the approved programs.

She feels that this is an expensive measure that is not only valuable but crucial because of the extremely competitive nature of her business. "A lot of people are really focused on making a profit," she comments, "and they sometimes lose track of the services they must provide." Because aesthetics has to be what Mabel calls a "totally customer-focused business," she believes the owner who tries to increase profits by skimping on training in the new products and services the public demands will soon not have any profits. She goes so far as to say that the "total customer focus" extends beyond the business goal of making a profit: "It is not just about making money. If that's your main focus, I don't think that you can be really successful in this kind of business."

In other words, training is one of those areas that proves the old adage, "You have to spend money to make money." In many modern business areas, customers, clients, and employees must feel that concern and resources are being put into quality: quality in skills, service, customer interface, and workplace environment. Training plays a crucial role here.

Individual Training and Development Requirements

Assessing the training and development requirements of the individual needs to be done on an ongoing basis and is a key component of the formal performance review process covered in Chapter 13, "Performance Reviews." There we saw that the process's key components are: determining the individual's development needs and working out a plan to meet them.

This formal review and the follow-up ongoing discussions need to address:

- the level of competency required for the job and whether the individual employee has reached that level

- what the person wants to do over the coming year or so (choices might include: wanting to expand knowledge and become more proficient in his or her current job, wanting to work on special assignments or in different areas of the business)

- what the individual hopes to accomplish in terms of business results

- an assessment of the person's current levels of competency and future requirements. This will reveal what gaps have to be filled to develop competencies to the required levels and allow the individual to meet future job requirements.

- the development of a plan, mutually arranged between management and the employee, to acquire the competencies that are now seen to be needed for the present and the future. This means a concrete and detailed plan that covers the methods for development, together with the actions and schedules that will lead to the goals set.

Once the training and development needs of both the organization and the individual have been determined through this process, it is time to think about how those needs are going to be filled.

WAYS OF IMPLEMENTING
TRAINING AND DEVELOPMENT

There are a number of ways that training and development plans can be implemented, each of which has its advantages and disadvantages. The methods chosen will be suggested by the specific circumstances and needs of the company. We will look at six types of training programs:

1. On-the-Job Training and Development

2. Computer-Based Training

3. Self-Study and Learning

4. Internal Training Programs

5. One-on-One Coaching

6. Outside Training Opportunities

Most of these approaches will probably require the company to provide time and money to allow individuals to ensure that they are able to develop themselves.

1. On-the-Job Training and Development

Most in-house training and development is done by learning while doing the job. This may involve specific training in particular skills or equipment being given by a colleague or supervisor. As we noted in an example above, David Marshall of Ergonomic Accessories Inc. has many of his full-time and contract staff train each other in various different specialties.

Advantages	Disadvantages
• The training is done during work hours.	• Training may be subject to interruptions that make it difficult for the individual to learn.
• Training is customized to the specific needs of the individual and his or her pace of learning.	• It may interfere with work in progress.
• The unique ways of the company are taught.	• The person doing the training may not be a good trainer.

2. Computer-Based Training

A number of companies are using computer-based programs such as CD-ROMs to train their staff. This is particularly useful for technology and computer application training but is being widely used by many organizations.

Advantages	Disadvantages
• It can be relatively inexpensive.	• If they are not a normal part of the business's operations, computers may have to be specially installed, and that is expensive.
• The training can be easily updated.	
• It offers flexibility of use, which is particularly valuable for shift people and those who work non-standard hours.	• Not everyone likes learning from a computer screen; many employees need some human interaction in order to learn effectively.
• Training can be done at the learning pace of the individual.	

3. Self-Study and Learning

Many organizations believe that individual employees are responsible for their own training and development. We heard David Anderson of CANATOM NPM express this view at the beginning of this chapter. However, such companies often have a policy of supporting employees in their own self-development efforts. David tells his employees, "I'm giving you the opportunity to develop. If you want to add to your skills by some training in your spare time, I will encourage you. We have some basis for reimbursing people for training they take in their own time, but we don't hire people and then spend six months training them."

As noted earlier, the development needs of an individual are best identified through the performance review process, and the second crucial step of this process is a plan to address these development needs. Such a plan can be a self-learning program that is put in place as a result of the performance review.

Self-study and training may take the form of reading, self-paced learning, or attendance in an external program at night or on weekends.

Advantages	Disadvantages
• Individuals who do this form of training are likely to be very committed and motivated to learn since it is done on their own time. • The learning acquired will fit in the employee's particular needs.	• Some employees may not learn quickly and thoroughly through a self-directed method.

4. Internal Training Programs

If there is a need for a number of people to learn a particular process or set of skills, it is often more cost effective to set up an internally run training program. Such programs can be delivered by either suppliers or internal experts.

Advantages	Disadvantages
• This type of training is specific to the company's training needs. • It is usually conducted by experts in a given field. • It does not interfere with production and work in progress. • People learn faster with fewer interruptions.	• Training is ineffective when an in-house expert is chosen who is not a skilled trainer. • Some people do not learn well when they are with their colleagues.

5. One-on-One Coaching

One-on-one coaching is an intensive and highly effective way of teaching specific skill sets and of training employees who do not respond well in group training situations or who may be slow learners. It is certainly becoming more popular as a development technique judging by the number of books and articles on the subject. This respected and worthwhile form of development has, unfortunately, become the latest fad in the United States. A friend of mine told me that having a development coach is currently in the same league as having a personal fitness trainer!

The coach is required to spend a specified amount of time with the trainee answering questions and providing advice. Coaches are frequently used by executives and managers to provide them with advice on running their business. It is usually helpful, if possible, to have a coach from outside the organization. Executives and managers find it extremely helpful to have people from outside because they themselves often need coaching in areas in which they are reluctant to admit their weaknesses and shortcomings to colleagues. They are not likely to be as honest and open with someone from inside the company and therefore may not come up with development plans that will help them improve. It is really helpful in these cases to bring in outside coaches if you want the group to develop.

In Chapter 17, "Advisory Boards," we will explore a more elaborate type of development coaching for a small business: the establishment of a board of advisers that is regularly consulted on questions of company strategy and operation.

Advantages	Disadvantages
• Since the coach is selected specifically to help an individual with his or her development needs, the likelihood of success is great.	• It takes longer than the other ways of training and development.
• The coach is usually someone with significant experience and therefore can quickly and effectively pass on knowledge.	• The coach will need to devote a specified and significant amount of time to the protégé.

6. Outside Training Opportunities

External training programs are effectively used when the needed skill is not to be found in the company and there is no one to teach it, or when a specific technical or professional designation (such as those for a professional engineer or accountant or trade designations) is required and must be earned through an accredited avenue. You may remember that David Haslam sent his plumbing apprentices to the local college so that they could get the required training.

Many suppliers of materials or services will provide courses for their clients, including training the employees of client companies. Sometimes the cost of these courses is built into the price charged for the materials or services, or there is a nominal charge.

Mabel Jakimtschuk of Sherwood Village Spa sends her staff on courses related to her industry, and in some cases, these are provided by the suppliers of the products she uses. She notes, "I send the employees on courses and I pay for the courses in, for example, nutrition and make-up techniques." In her business field, personal aesthetics, Mabel finds educational offerings for her staff members "mostly from individual companies that sell different products and provide different courses or seminars. It's usually a four, five, or six-day course, but some are longer. For example, reflexology is a six-month course." It's not unusual for her to close the business for a day while everyone takes a company-sponsored seminar on new products.

Advantages	Disadvantages
• This type of training can bring in up-to-date knowledge from external educational sources. • It enables employees to meet other people from similar firms, which, in itself, can provide even more learning through communications about similar experiences. • It is usually conducted by expert and seasoned trainers.	• Employees may have to take time off work to attend. • Courses may not meet the specific needs of an individual since they are designed for general training and development requirements.

PROBLEM EMPLOYEES: PERFORMANCE IMPROVEMENT

The best way to deal with problem employees is to prevent the problem from developing, and the place to start is in recruitment. Taking care with each new hire is the surest guarantee the entrepreneur has that the costly and time-consuming process of dealing with problem employees can be avoided. The preceding chapters (12 to 14) outlined reliable methods for integrating new hires: thorough orientation and continuing emphasis on free and open communications, regular performance reviews that rely on clearly stated goals and objectives, and employee access to needed training and development. Sometimes, however, despite all your best efforts, something starts to go wrong.

Common indicators of a performance problem include:

- missed or unsatisfactorily completed objectives
- missed deadlines and timetables
- poor quality work
- a demonstrable lack of required skills
- unacceptable behaviour towards other people in the company or clients and suppliers

PERFORMANCE IMPROVEMENT: A CASE HISTORY

When a problem is uncovered, a manager must act decisively. Kieran O'Briain of Kee Transport outlined some concrete examples of how he handles problems with employees. "A while back we had a problem with drivers not completing their paperwork. There were something like 40 drivers who weren't handing it in. I called each office and asked how many of these guys had had a one-on-one orientation. We found out that seven drivers had had a one-to-one. So those seven got penalized as they were told they would be. The rest of them were not. We paid them anyway, and then arranged to have a conversation with each one. So, slowly but surely, we got the message through."

TIPS AND TRAPS FOR MANAGERS

A brief summary of what to do and what not to do when trying to solve an employee problem:

Traps	Tips
Condone inappropriate behaviour.	Correct inappropriate behaviour.
Act on assumptions and gossip.	Gather facts.
Be judgemental.	Stay objective.
Act informally.	Document all aspects of issue.
Avoid talking problem over with employee.	Listen to the employee's side.
Hurry through issue.	Make time for thorough assessment.

THE FIVE-STEP PERFORMANCE IMPROVEMENT PROCESS

Here is a five-step program I have used, and encourage my clients to use, when dealing with problem employees. The performance improvement process (PIP) is a positive process for action to correct a performance or behaviour problem with measurable performance or behaviour targets and agreed-upon time frames. PIP is not a disciplinary measure but rather a proactive way to encourage an employee to correct behaviour or to improve deteriorating performance.

The five steps of PIP are:

1. Fact Gathering

2. Informing the Employee about the Process

3. Setting a Timetable for Improvement

4. Documenting the Progress of Change

5. Judging the Process and Choosing a Response

The following is an example of a situation in which a performance improvement process was used and outlines the steps that were followed. These will then be discussed in more detail in the following pages.

A professional services firm hired a person in a relatively senior position, and while this employee's performance was initially good, over the past few months, a series of performance and behavioural problems surfaced. The person was demanding a salary increase because he considered that he was underpaid in relation to other employees. It transpired that the individual was having personal financial difficulties and wanted the money to overcome them.

Next, the person's work performance was slipping and the responsibilities, accountabilities, and required results were not being achieved. Thirdly, this person was becoming very abusive towards other colleagues and indulging in screaming matches in the corridor. Finally, the individual's punctuality was not very good. He was arriving late, taking two-hour lunches, and going home early. Why, you might ask, would the company wish to put this person through a performance improvement process?

The owner/entrepreneur of the company judged that the employee did indeed have potential, and preferred to take him through the performance improvement process rather than fire him immediately.

Thus, the steps taken were first to document and gather facts about the specific problems that had been noted. It was necessary to get specific examples because nothing had been put on the employee's file to date. Once these facts had been gathered, the employee was informed about the areas in which he was not meeting the performance requirements and told that he was going to be put into the performance improvement process. A timetable for improvement was set. The employee was given one month to show improvement in all the areas noted—i.e., achieving the required results, coming in on time, and ceasing abuse towards colleagues.

Each week the individual was to meet with his manager and document the process of change. This meant that while the process was going on, the owner/manager had to acquire evidence from colleagues that there was indeed change.

After the fifth step, which is still in process, the manager/owner will have to decide whether or not the individual has achieved the required results. If he does achieve the required results 100 per cent, he will remain with the company. But if the results are 75 per cent or less, the individual will be fired.

Step One: Fact Gathering

The first step is for the manager to meet with the employee and gather as much relevant information as possible about possible causes for the work problem. Questions to ask would include the following:

- Is the employee fully informed of the goals set for the job?
- Does the employee have the necessary facilities and equipment to do the job?
- Does the employee lack skills and training necessary to do the job?
- Does the employee have difficulty with specific aspects of the company's culture or operating rules?
- Does the employee have difficulty with a co-worker or supervisor?
- Are there family or personal problems affecting performance?
- Does the employee have health problems?

A frank discussion with the employee may satisfy the manager that the problem can be solved quickly and without further intervention. It may be, for example, that standards for a position have changed and the employee has not been told, so that all that is needed is a brief review of the new standards. Perhaps a reorganization of management assignments has led to a confusion about job responsibilities for this employee, and some clarification about a position's duties will be enough to end the work problem. Or the problem might be that an employee may need additional training on a new piece of equipment or support in dealing with a family crisis.

If the manager and employee agree that the problem has been resolved, there is no need to go on with the formal process. If, however, no agreement is reached, the manager should proceed through the remaining four steps of PIP as presented below.

Step Two: Informing the Employee about the Process

The manager decides on a course of action that would be a satisfactory corrective to the problem. Having decided on a course of action, the manager should notify the employee that a formal performance improvement process is about to begin. The employee should be told:

• why the performance improvement process is being implemented, with specific examples provided of unacceptable behaviour and/or performance

• how the improper behaviour and/or performance has impacted the company's productivity

• what specific actions the employee is expected to undertake to correct the behaviour and/or performance issue

Step Three: Setting a Timetable for Improvement

The employee should be given not only directives about what changes in performance must be made, but also a specific timetable for making the changes.

The time frame of the performance improvement process depends on the scope of the problem. It probably should last for at least two weeks but no longer than three months. Interim target dates should be set for accomplishing specific improvements, and the manager and employee should meet on these target dates for follow-up consultations.

Step Four: Documenting the Progress of Change

At each target date, the manager and employee should meet, and the manager should document the results of the session. A copy should be given to the employee and another placed in the employee's file. The manager has to get evidence from colleagues and make his or her own observations to ensure that the required results are being met. These need to be reviewed on a weekly basis with the employee and noted in the employee's file. This can be quite a tedious process, but if one is determined to be fair and to use the performance improvement process, this is a very important step.

Step Five: Judging the Process and Choosing a Response

At the end of the period set for improving performance, a manager has to choose among three options:

A. Successful Conclusion

B. Extension Required

C. Unsuccessful Conclusion

Option A. Successful Conclusion

If the employee has met the required objectives, the performance improvement process concludes, and the employee remains in his or her current role in good standing. The manager documents the successful outcome and distributes copies to the employee and to the employee's official personnel file.

Option B. Extension Required

If the employee has not met the performance improvement objectives but has shown significant improvement in behaviour and/or performance, the process may be extended for a defined period of time. The manager documents the extension and distributes copies to the employee and the employee's official personnel file.

Option C. Unsuccessful Conclusion

If the employee has not met the objectives and has not made significant improvement in behaviour and/or performance, the next step would be to begin the termination process. This is discussed fully in the next chapter, "Termination Procedures."

Although the manager and employee must work together if the performance improvement process is to succeed, the entrepreneur should recognize just how much of the responsibility for this process resides with management. The manager must:

• prepare the detailed PIP and present it to the employee

• meet the employee regularly for progress reports

• maintain documentation

• judge the outcome of the process

• ensure that business needs are met throughout

I recommend that a small business operator seek help from an HR practitioner, either in-house or an external consultant, when attempting to resolve an employee problem through a formal performance improvement process.

CHAPTER SIXTEEN

TERMINATION PROCEDURES

This chapter will look at the two forms of termination: voluntary and involuntary. The first occurs when an individual quits and the second when an individual is fired.

VOLUNTARY TERMINATION

Voluntary termination takes place when an employee chooses to leave your company for whatever reason. When this happens, the employee must give notice to the employer in order to allow you time to find and train a replacement. In some cases, you may wish the employee to leave immediately rather than work out their notice. This could be because staying on may be destructive to other employees, or you may not want them to have access to restricted and confidential information.

Notice Period

As Margaret Kerr and JoAnn Kurtz note in their book, *Make It Legal*, some provinces have employment standards legislation that sets out the exact notice period—usually one or two weeks—that an employee must give an employer.[1] The notice period may also have been specified in the offer letter that the employee was given when hired.

Once the employee has given notice, you will have to decide whether you want him or her to work out their notice period or leave the company immediately. Either way, you will have to pay that person the salary or wages and benefits for the notice period.

Exit Interview

It can be useful to conduct an exit interview with an employee who quits to find out why he or she has chosen to leave. You may want to do this yourself or get someone else from within the company to conduct the interview. The situation may warrant hiring someone neutral from outside the firm to speak to the departing employee in order to elicit a more honest response.

People who can conduct exit interviews might be external consultants or your own office manager or chief financial officer. Here are the questions that need to be asked in the exit interview:

- Why are you leaving the company?
- What is the new position offering you that you're not getting here?
- Describe your supervisor's style. Did this have anything to do with your decision to leave the company?
- Did you have sufficient training to do your job here?
- What was it about first joining the company that excited you and made you want to join the company?
- What are your salary, wages, benefits, and bonuses in your new position?
- How were you recruited?

Asking these questions gives you a feel for why the employee is leaving, and you may be able to correct some things. It also gives you a chance to find out what your competition is doing in terms of making jobs more attractive, compensation offers, and what methods of recruitment they're using.

The exit interview provides you with a chance to find out why the employee decided to leave and may uncover issues that may have caused that person to leave. These may be things you want to address in order to prevent others from going the same route. Whoever is doing the exit interview needs to ask for feedback about the company as a whole and about the position and the department in particular.

INVOLUNTARY TERMINATION

Though it is usually in the best interests of a company to see that every employee is successful in his or her job, there will be times when it is better to cut one's losses and fire an employee. Involuntary termination occurs when you have to fire a person even though he or she does not want to leave. Many employers find this a very difficult course of action and often try to avoid the responsibility. This may be due to the fact that they dislike conflict and will avoid it at any cost. Or it can be because they don't want to be seen as the bad guy.

Even the toughest of entrepreneurs will put off firing an employee—and many consider themselves too soft-hearted in this area. They often do not act quickly enough—if at all—to remove an employee whose performance has been unsatisfactory or whose negative attitude has been disruptive.

As Rick Spence writes, "Putting off the inevitable can be a deadly mistake in small, growing companies built on teamwork and attitude. Failure to eliminate one bad apple will not only permit the rot to continue, it actively encourages further decay; morale among other team members declines as they perceive management's inability to deal with the problem. In admitting their error, some PROFIT 100 entrepreneurs confess that they often handed off the dirty work to others. Whether you do it yourself or through others, the important thing is that it must be done. Proactive firing is at least as important as creative hiring and inspiring others to work."[2]

In the long run it is better for both the individual and the organization to terminate quickly and properly. Employees usually know or sense when something is not going well and often feel excluded from meetings or social events and functions. They are often just waiting for the axe to fall. Hence, delaying the decision can be very stressful for the individual, for the manager, and for everyone involved. Other employees in the company usually know when a colleague is not up to scratch and can feel the effects on their own performance and that of the company.

If the ineffective person is not let go, it can have a very negative impact on productivity and morale. When a termination is necessary, quick action benefits all involved even though preparing for the deed is not a pleasant task.

The reasons for involuntary terminations fall into three categories:

- Business Reasons
- Performance and Attitude Reasons
- Just Cause Reasons

Business Reasons

Involuntary terminations are sometimes due to business reasons. Your business may not have done as well financially as you expected, which may mean that you are not able to keep all the employees you had originally hired.

Or, your business may have changed since its inception, having moved into different areas or offering goods and services that are superior to those offered at the outset. When such changes occur, there are often employees who do not have or cannot develop the competence, skills, and knowledge for the new business requirements. They will need to be replaced with people who do have the required competencies to run the business now and in the future.

Performance and Attitude Reasons

The second set of reasons has to do with an individual's performance or attitude. The employee may not be performing to the standards you require or may not be achieving the required results. You may already have taken the employee through the performance improvement process described in Chapter 15 and found that the individual's performance has still not improved sufficiently. At this point, the decision must be made to let the employee go.

In other cases, an employee may simply have a bad attitude towards the job, the company, or work in general. This can have very negative consequences, such as poor morale, and the situation may demand removal of the person from his or her position before further damage is done to the company or other employees.

Just Cause Reasons

The third category of reasons for termination is just cause. While just cause is a legal reason for requiring the person to leave immediately and is not quite in the same category as business reasons or performance and attitude reasons, it will still nonetheless be covered as a reason for involuntary termination. Just cause allows you to fire a person and have him or her leave the company immediately. In cases of just cause, you do not have to give any advance notice or pay any money in lieu of notice. Just cause is a term under law; as Kerr and Kurtz note in *Make It Legal*,[3] the following reasons are considered just cause for firing an employee:

- dishonesty towards the employer, including theft or embezzlement

- other criminal activity of a serious nature on or off the job, whether or not the employee is convicted of, or charged with, a crime

- insubordination or disobedience, including refusal to obey reasonable orders or talking back to superiors

- disruption of corporate culture by continued bad behaviour towards other employees, customers, or suppliers, including rudeness, shouting, or sexual or racial harassment

- drunkenness or drug abuse that the employee has been warned about and that affects the employee's work (but human rights legislation requires an employer to "accommodate" first)

- repeated absences or lateness without a reasonable medical or personal excuse

- incompetence or carelessness in the performance of the job that continues in spite of warnings

- long-term physical or mental illness that prevents the employee from carrying out the job not withstanding the fact that reasonable accommodation has been made

- conflict of interest with the employer—for example, competing with you, taking business away from you, or using your property for personal benefit

Where the termination is for just cause, only in the case of dishonesty and criminal activity can you fire the employee immediately for wrongdoing. In all the other cases noted above, you have to give the employee a warning and an opportunity to improve. It is only after that behaviour does not improve in response to warnings that you can fire without notice or without any form of payment in lieu of notice.

In considering a firing for just cause, then, you will have to know the law with regard to any specifications about warnings and accommodations for the particular cause in question. And you will have to document your actions in a provable manner.

Firing without Just Cause

Suppose you want to fire someone because of changing business circumstances, inappropriate behaviour such as a bad attitude, or failure to meet performance expectations. How do you do it? You can certainly terminate someone for these reasons but at a cost to your business. You must give reasonable notice of termination and pay the employee for the statutory notice period. That period is usually one or two weeks, depending on the local provincial employment standards legislation.

> Kerr and Kurtz outlined the legislation with regard to notice requirements in *Make it Legal:*[4]
>
> • An employee who has worked for you for less than the minimum period of time (depending on the province, a period between one and six months) is not entitled to any notice.
>
> • An employee who has worked for you for more than six months (again, depending on the province) is entitled to one week's (in some provinces, two weeks') notice in the first year, then one week's notice for each subsequent year he or she has worked for you, up to a maximum of eight weeks (in a few provinces, the maximum notice period is only two to four weeks). This notice must be given in writing.

Paying More than the Statutory Minimum

As we have seen, provincial legislation established the notice period across the country, but in some cases, the employer may wish to pay the departing employee more than the statutory minimum. For example, in cases in which the employee feels wronged, this could avoid a lawsuit and would also ensure that the employee leaves on a positive note and does not bad-mouth your company in the community or to other potential employees.

While some employers do pay more than the statutory minimum just to be seen to be fair and to stop possible criticism of the company, it is not always a good idea because it may well be seen as a form of admission of wrongdoing. Although some companies are prepared to be quite generous in their settlements, it all depends on the affordability of such packages and the direction that the company wishes to take. It is well worth consulting a lawyer in this case to determine what should be done and what the implications are of paying more or staying with the legal minimum.

Leaving the Company Immediately

What if you do not want the employee to continue to work in the company once you've given him or her notice? You can ask the individual to leave immediately, but you still have to pay his or her salary or wages and benefits throughout the relevant notice period.

If you hire a person on probation who proves unsatisfactory, you may terminate him or her at the end of that probation period without having to give notice or payment in lieu of notice.

Replacing the Terminated Individual

In cases where you are about to terminate someone, you will have to take steps to replace him or her. It is often very difficult to keep the fact of termination confidential because you need to get the search under way for a replacement. In such a case, you will need to source your contacts and work your network to find out if any appropriate candidates are available and at the same time, be confidential about why you're doing such a search.

HR WISDOM ON TERMINATION

Over the past few years, several things have emerged from experience regarding termination in the contemporary business environment. By following these guidelines, you can allow an employee to leave with dignity and a sense of worth and at the same time, protect the reputation and operations of your company.

THE SEVEN RULES FOR TERMINATION

1. Do not terminate at the beginning of the work week. The person may be forced to stay at home an entire week while family and friends are at work, and this may leave him or her feeling depressed and unhappy.

2. Do not terminate at the very end of the work week. The individual will then have to go home and face family and friends with the news rather than having a day or two to prepare himself or herself for the change.

3. Do not terminate close to public holidays or on someone's birthday. This will certainly leave the person feeling low and may ruin both family and friends' holidays as well.

4. Ensure that the termination is done in private in order to spare the individual being terminated, and other employees as well, any additional grief.

5. Make sure that once the date of leaving is set, the employee pays off any outstanding accounts and loans. Collect any company property such as IDs, keys, passes, credit cards, equipment, or tools.

6. Make sure you have stopped authorization for purchase orders. I can cite a recent case of a departing employee, whose purchasing privileges were not formally terminated, ordering computer equipment. The individual subsequently bought equipment and disappeared with it, leaving the company responsible for payment. It is absolutely essential to terminate formally any authorization for purchase orders the departing employee might have.

7. If appropriate, offer a letter of reference, and assist the individual in finding other employment. Even though you've let him or her go, you may still have respect for the individual's skills and abilities and feel that you can honestly offer a positive recommendation to another company or employer.

COMMUNICATION TO OTHERS

Employers often avoid telling their staff, customers, or clients that someone has left the company, and this can lead to all kinds of speculation and rumour. Your silence creates a mystery, and employee morale can be seriously damaged from the resulting wild guesses and gossip.

Informing Other Employees

It is very important to tell other employees what has happened and why, within reason. Too often, once an individual has been dismissed, it is as if they never existed. Fellow employees are told nothing and soon begin to wonder where the employee is and what has happened to him or her. Frequently, uninformed employees will develop the belief that dismissal was due to business reasons such as lower-than-expected profits or revenues. The remaining employees then are likely to wonder if they will be affected and perhaps be the next casualties of the supposed business downturn. Morale can be badly affected. It is crucial to explain what has happened and why and explain possible future impacts on employment.

If a senior person has been terminated, employees will wonder if the person is going to be replaced, who their next colleague is going to be, and what impact the change will have on them. So you must let them know what's going to happen with the position.

Thus, it is essential to communicate with all employees as soon as possible after the termination. This can be done in person, by e-mail, or by a letter, putting as positive a spin as possible on the event. It should cover such points as:

• when the employee left

• why he or she left, whether to pursue other opportunities or for just cause

• an expression of thanks to the employee for his or her contribution in all cases in which there was no dishonesty or other just cause for termination

• an assurance, if possible, about the state of the business and whether other positions are going to remain stable. (Of course, this may not be honestly possible if the termination was in fact due to the pressures of a tough economic period.)

Here are some examples of good and bad forms of communications to employees that someone has left the company.

An example of bad communications would be, "Jane/John Doe has left the company." This can be very upsetting to the remaining employees because they know of no reason why the employee has left, where they're going, or even when they left. This is the kind of communications that should be avoided.

A better form of communications is, "I wish to inform you that Jane/John Doe has left the company to pursue other interests on [date]. Please join me in wishing [her or him] every success in [his or her] future endeavours." This allows the individual to go out with dignity, even if they have been fired, and it also shows a little more compassion towards the existing employees.

Informing Customers and Suppliers

It is also important to inform customers and suppliers about an individual's departure. Just as it is the case with employees, customers or other clients may wonder what has happened, and if you don't tell them the truth, rumours may spread regarding the reason for the departure, where the person has gone, and the like. It is best to contact personally every customer with whom the individual may have dealt and briefly mention that he or she has left the company. If the person has gone elsewhere, you can relay that information, but I recommend simply stating that the individual has left the organization. That in itself will prevent unnecessary rumours and speculation.

> There are three principles regarding termination:
>
> 1. Act decisively and quickly.
> 2. Employees who are terminated need to be treated with dignity and respect.
> 3. Consideration must also be given to the effect the termination will have on other employees and on customers.

TERMINATION PAPERWORK

A number of things need to happen once an employee has left the company, whether by voluntary or involuntary termination. Four of them are discussed:

1. Record of Employment
2. Pay
3. Benefits Coverage
4. References

1. Record of Employment

First, a Record of Employment form has to be completed within five days of the employee's leaving the company. These forms, together with instructions on how to complete them, are available from Human Resources Development Canada (HRDC). A copy of the form has to be given to the employee once it is completed, with one copy sent to HRDC.

2. Pay

Any outstanding wages and salaries, together with termination pay and vacation pay, have to be forwarded to the employee, usually within a few days of the employee's last working day. The exact time varies from province to province, depending on employment standards legislation.

3. Benefits Coverage

The insurance carrier must be notified that the individual has left the company and if there has been an agreement to continue with any form of benefits coverage after the termination.

4. References

The final concern you may have is whether to provide a reference for the employee as he or she begins to look for another position. Many employers will say only that the person worked for the company and provide the dates of employment. They may be concerned that if they say more, they can be sued. Other companies will provide more detail because they know that the negative information they may give about the employee is true; some companies can honestly provide positive assessments of terminated employees and will give references because they have no desire to prevent the individual from getting another job. The decision is entirely up to the employer and depends on the situation. If you can substantiate your facts in providing a negative assessment, there is no cause to fear a legal action.

PART FIVE

SPECIAL ISSUES

We have left discussion of three special situations facing the small business operator for this final part: advisory boards, planning for succession, and hiring consultants. Chapter 17, "Advisory Boards," discusses the growing practice among entrepreneurs of organizing mentors, outside experts, and others into a panel of advisers to provide advice on the development of the business. Chapter 18, "Planning for Management Succession," offers methods—often neglected in single-owner, family-owned, and small companies—for providing a successor and preparing for transition. Chapter 19, "Hiring a Consultant," tells how to recognize when the management team has outgrown its abilities to deal with specific issues and needs to acquire competent and experienced help from outside the organization.

CHAPTER SEVENTEEN

ADVISORY BOARDS

An entrepreneur must be, first and foremost, self-reliant, but there are times when the best thing you can do for yourself is to find someone you trust and ask for advice. Sometimes the person approached is a mentor or a long-time friend in the same industry. In family businesses, you may consult with a parent or sibling who has had years of experience in the very position you currently hold. Small business operators are also likely to seek counsel from the same resource persons outside the firm who provide them with essential services, including accounting, insurance, legal support, banking, and investment management. In fact, many small business experts say that entrepreneurial success depends as much on the entrepreneur's ability to develop a team of reliable advisers as it does on his or her individual qualities.

WHAT ARE ADVISORY BOARDS?

One way to increase the benefit of such informal advice gathering is to organize the individuals you frequently consult into an advisory board.

An advisory board is a group set up to meet regularly to review business plans and new projects and also to give feedback, as needed, whenever special questions arise. Such an advisory board differs from a public company's board of directors in a number of ways. First, an advisory board is not a legal requirement for a private company, while a board of directors is a legal requirement for a public company. Second, advisory board members do not assume any legal or financial responsibility, while members of a board of directors may be held accountable both for the company's illegal actions and for its failures to meet financial obligations to employees and stockholders. Third, a board of director's responsibilities to the corporation are frequently set out in company statutes; this is rarely done with an advisory board.

Like members of a board of directors, advisory board members frequently are paid for their services. Many experts suggest that the board members should receive a monthly fee as a guarantee that timely expert advice is available when needed, perhaps even to avert a costly crisis intervention, and also as a way to match the expense with the company's regular cash flow.

Statistics aren't available, but small business counsellors, like Joan Berta of CAFE and Lynda Bowles of Deloitte and Touche, agree that advisory boards are increasingly popular among Canadian small businesses, and that is my own impression from my consulting work.

According to Jonathan Kovacheff of Kovacheff Consulting Group Inc., "I've never seen a corporation that has properly formed an advisory board that has regretted the decision." He identifies two services that advisory boards can provide for small and medium-size businesses:

1. expertise not available in-house

2. advice on governance issues—that is, questions arising from overseeing company growth and development

TO BOARD OR NOT TO BOARD

None of the entrepreneurs I interviewed had organized an advisory board, although most were familiar with the idea and some had already begun considering forming one; many of them said that their businesses were too small and/or too new to warrant one. They relied on a variety of sources for expertise.

> Susan Niczowski of Summer Fresh Salads Inc.: "We have no advisory board per se and get our advice by basically talking to people. Nothing prevents asking questions."
>
> David Haslam of Presidential Plumbing Ltd.: "If I need banking advice, I have to go to my account manager. I guess I'm very fortunate that the friendships I've created over the years have provided me with sources of great advice; because of this, I'm able to steal little bits and pieces from other businesses."
>
> Mabel Jakimtschuk of Sherwood Village Spa: "My greatest source of expertise is reading, but I also have a lot of clients who are business consultants, and I share my ideas with them."
>
> Karen Flavelle of Purdy's Chocolates: "We have been talking about having a board of advisors for probably ten years. We've talked about it, but frankly, I don't really feel the need because I belong to a personal advisory group that is part of the Canadian Association for Family Enterprise (CAFE) and to YPO (Young Presidents Organization). Thus I have other resources that I depend on."

Knowing When to Say When

Only Kieran O'Briain of Kee Transport said he was actively considering the formation of an advisory board. His interest grows out of a problem he encountered in getting timely financial advice about a new venture. Accustomed to relying for advice on his father and his father's old business partner, Kieran had circulated to them and to his accountant copies of a plan for a new venture. Then he began to wait. He explains: "So, I just put together a business plan for a venture I'm doing in New Brunswick for my warehousing business. The accountant is supposed to be coming in next week. It's stuff like that. My accountant's supposed to be here this week and he isn't here. No phone call. No nothing."

Kieran hopes that an advisory board might help with routine functions as well as special projects, but he is uncertain about how to put a board together. He asks, "Those kinds of advising stuff—obviously my accountant gives me advice from his perspective, my father gives me the boardroom stuff, but should the other board member be a legal person or should it be one of my customers? One of them offered to be on the board, but should you have a customer on there? Who would make up a typical advisory team, and where do you find them? And what do you pay them? Do you pay them anything? How long does the board go on?"

THE FIVE KEY QUESTIONS

The discussion that follows examines five key questions about advisory boards:

1. When Is It Time to Set Up an Advisory Board?
2. What Is the Advisory Board Expected to Do?
3. Who Should Sit on the Advisory Board?
4. Should the Advisory Board Be Paid?
5. What Is the Lifespan of an Advisory Board?

I received valuable material on several of these questions from Jonathan Kovacheff, who was drawing on his consulting practice as well as his years as a lawyer and university teacher. Because of her experiences both as an informal adviser to entrepreneurs and as an observer of many companies at the moment of their decision to form an advisory board, Lynda Bowles can help us with the timing question. Joan Berta's work with CAFE gives an insight into how many family businesses gain expert advice through an alternative to forming their own advisory group, CAFE's Personal Advisory Groups. She can help us with the question that is often an important one for Canadian small business: What special problems do family businesses encounter when setting up an advisory board?

1. When Is It Time to Set Up an Advisory Board?

Advisory boards are most often formed when a start-up business begins to grow, and the operator wonders how to gain access to expert information on a range of subjects crucial to expansion such as how to raise capital, how to get good financial planning help, and who to approach for help in entering a new market. Jonathan Kovacheff explains, "When you're starting up a business, or growing a business, advisers can help you uncover opportunities, either routes into the capital markets or new markets. It's that expertise you're trying to tap." He goes on, "I think the needs vary depending on the type of business and the quality of the business owner. If it's a start-up and a first-time owner with someone who doesn't have a lot of experience, what they really need is functional expertise. They need help with such things as how to run the business, budgeting business planning, and strategic planning. They may also need help with management capability and access to markets and capital. So there are a variety of things the start-up person is looking for just to get them up the learning curve."

Lynda Bowles sees advisory boards in much the same way. "I just ran across two or three companies lately that are developing advisory boards. These companies are at the stage where they're trying to grow, trying to get some additional capital. The companies are past cottage industry stage, and they are serious about growing. In some cases the owners are willing to make a personal investment in the company by mortgaging their houses, for example. They realize that they don't have all the expertise they need to make the company successful, and they can't afford to purchase that expertise."

Lynda Bowles, who is often asked by women entrepreneurs to review ideas and business plans, also believes that setting up an advisory board is more typical of women than of men because "most women are willing to help other women. They do not mind talking about things and sharing ideas." According to Bowles, women are "more consultative" by nature and "are not trying to do it all themselves."

The typical board organized by a woman entrepreneur, Bowles says, is made up of "a lawyer, a finance person, a marketing person, and a sales person."

2. What Is the Advisory Board Expected to Do?

An entrepreneur generally first considers forming an advisory board because of specific operational problems; for example, Kieran O'Briain wanted fast advice on the finances of setting up a new venture. The small business owner may want to expand into a new market or experiment with a new product line. Rather than limiting the advisory board at start-up to such specific questions, Lynda Bowles recommends a general overview of the company's operations. "When developing an advisory board, the owner identifies their weaknesses. The meetings of the board could include a review of the business plan, assistance on identifying alternative financing arrangements, assessing the marketing plan, and reviewing the cost structure with a view to controlling costs."

In addition, an advisory board can be a valuable tool in developing a long-term company strategy. The small business operator needs help on what Jonathan Kovacheff calls "governance issues," such as management succession, especially because "small businesses generally don't understand the difference between governance and operational matters." Setting up an advisory board encourages the entrepreneur to spend time on planning rather than just putting out fires.

Governance Issues

Setting up an advisory board can be a valuable aid to the entrepreneur whose firm is beginning to grow, especially if the advisory board is used to develop the ability to plan for the long term and to assess business decisions in light of their impact on the corporation as a whole—that is, if it is used to address governance issues.

Many small business operators, however, tend to push "global thinking" into the future, perhaps for the time when the company goes public and a board of directors with fiduciary responsibility will become a legal requirement. Until then, they feel, an informal board is less complicated to work with. Concerns about legal requirements, such as annual filings or audited statements, can be handled by a consulting corporate counsel.

But small businesses have governance issues. According to Jonathan Kovacheff, "Stewarding the company often involves internal controls. Thus small, new firms need help on monitoring all the risks and opportunities in the organizations as a whole. They need to set up an overarching structure to take care of the corporation." Learning to work with an advisory board can help the entrepreneur with one of the biggest challenges of the job, which is to provide leadership and direction for the company. Setting up an advisory board early, with a mandate to comment both on operations and governance issues, has two other advantages for the entrepreneur. First, it can be a stepping stone towards the formation of the board of directors when the time comes to take the company public. Many advisory board members are likely to be suitable candidates for a directorship as well, and their familiarity with the firm from years of working with it will be an asset in future consultations. Second, an advisory board can help the entrepreneur with the difficult transition from thinking only as a business operator to thinking as a business owner. Entrepreneurs need to give up doing everything for themselves and "start adding some rigour at the top of the organization," Jonathan explains. An advisory board is an excellent tool for adding structure to planning and decision making.

3. Who Should Sit on the Advisory Board?

An advisory board may grow directly from the informal advice-gathering network that most entrepreneurs instinctively develop or from a more formal search. The first step, however, is to treat the process as a business decision. "I don't think that your advisory board should be your friends," Lynda Bowles warns. "You need a business approach." Of her own informal advice sessions, she explains, "When I say these are my friends, they're not my personal friends; they're business friends, which is different."

Many small business experts suggest that a logical starting point is with the short list of those outside experts already familiar with your business: your bank manager, accountant, lawyer, perhaps a business consultant you have brought in fairly regularly. The value added of the advisory board structure is that these individual counsellors begin to share ideas.

The entrepreneur has other options in seeking members for an advisory board, according to Jonathan Kovacheff: "There are a variety of mechanisms. The typical sole owner of a corporation will approach, through the networks they have, people who are usually wealthy individuals, or people who don't have to work for a living, who really want to give back to small businesses. They will make a list of people who might want to mentor them. They will often approach people who come from their industry—a retired CEO or a senior vice-president of operations or something, who is looking for some place to work and help out. There is a huge pool of people who have just retired." He cautions, however, that "access to that pool is difficult if you don't have the network."

Larry Ginsberg, writing in *The Globe and Mail*, suggests, "Start by making a list of successful business people in your industry—people you respect and who appear to have achieved their goals. Tell them how much you respect what they have accomplished. Then ask if they would mind telling you who their key advisers are. If they view you as a direct competitor, they may choose not to share this information. But if they believe you are an up-and-comer, they may be flattered and willing to refer certain advisers to you."[1]

Ginsberg gives a checklist of other people to ask: "friends, former school contacts, current advisers, and business colleagues, including customers and suppliers." What you're looking for, he says, is "the chemistry or fit between entrepreneur and the adviser. If owners don't feel comfortable with prospective advisers, they should not employ them no matter how strong their credentials."

4. Should the Advisory Board Be Paid?

Entrepreneurs may wonder why they should consider paying for what they might be able to get for free, especially from long-time friends and mentors. But many experts look at it another way: putting an expert on retainer probably means getting top-notch advice at a reduced fee; it also means spreading out the cost of consulting, which helps cash flow, and it means you have someone to call in case of an emergency who is already well versed in your business.

Besides, you may need a very specific type of expertise. Jonathan Kovacheff explains. "As the business gets more mature and has hired good people and has external people working with them, they will require more specific expertise on the advisory council. For instance, if they are a $30-million company now and want to penetrate the Asian market, they want someone who knows how to do this. They will ask someone to sit on their board for 20 to 30 days per year, which is much cheaper than paying a consultant to give this advice. Thus, the structure of the advisory board will depend on what the owner/operator needs at a certain point in their development."

5. What Is the Lifespan of an Advisory Board?

A successful advisory board, one that has supplied expertise on operational questions and also given direction on governance issues, should grow in the direction of a public company's board of directors. Jonathan Kovacheff explains, "As the corporation moves towards a deal to become a public company, it has to transform the board or the council into more of a fiduciary body. By law and by the TSE standards, you have to have a 'fully functioning fiduciary board' ready to go to close that deal. Many times, that will be a condition of the agreement, particularly if it's public equity or a large pension fund that's going to be an investor."

He suggests, then, that as the advisory board grows, it should adapt not only by bringing in new experts, possibly attracting them with higher fees, but also by "bringing in some of that governance discipline to a truly fiduciary board or stewardship board."

FAMILY-RUN BUSINESSES AND ADVISORY BOARDS

Small family businesses need the same sort of advisers that other small businesses do: financial consultants, experts in opening up new markets, veteran managers, and so on. In addition, their advisory boards should probably include family lawyers and tax planners. According to Jonathan Kovacheff, family businesses routinely face special problems in two areas: having family members working closely together and providing for an orderly management succession.

Succession issues often dictate additions to the advisory boards of family-run businesses: advisers with expertise in this area, including tax planners and lawyers, are likely to sit alongside "the functional experts, the market experts, the operational experts" we've already seen in discussing advisory boards in general, according to Jonathan Kovacheff.

"The family-run business is like any other business in the sense that it needs all the things we just talked about, but when you think about a family-run business, there are really three buckets of issues they've got to think about, as opposed to just one." These are:

1. the business itself

2. succession

3. family issues growing out of family members working together

The last two issues, though, call for specialized attention.

The Special Circumstances of Family Businesses

"In a family-owned business," according to Jonathan, "there are family-related business issues. These are really around succession, tax planning, and buyout clauses that impact the business and require some mechanism for control, monitoring, and expertise. Many times, they'll use outside experts—lawyers or financial advisers—to give them expertise. That's fine, as long as it's structured properly. But some corporations have moved in this area by having their advisers come from a pool that also understands the issues of a family-run business.

"The third area that needs to be considered is how you get along with your siblings, and spousal questions also need a way to be addressed. Some people, for instance, take family counselling to get through these issues."

Going to CAFE for Advice

Joan Berta offers another perspective on helping family businesses get expert business advice. For some years, her organization, the Canadian Association of Family Enterprise (CAFE), has been running personal advisory groups (PAGs), which bring together business experts and family business managers together in a helpful exchange. This exchange is especially beneficial, according to Joan, because family businesses often operate in isolation: "The only way they know anything is done is the way it's done in their own organization. That's one of the very useful tools of our personal advisory groups."

She describes a typical group: "Eight to 12 individuals, with no two competing businesses in the group and no two family members in the same group." The regular meetings mean that each family business gets its own "personal and business support group. So when you walk into that room—you meet once a month—there are two very strong rules: number one is commitment, and number two is confidentiality. And you can discuss anything about your business and anything about your family.

"In my PAG, we review people's marketing plans and their business plans. We help them put a sales pitch together; we helped somebody put a catalogue together for their product. Somebody's helping us all get our Web pages set up. Then you at least get a benefit from these eight or ten people and how things are done in their companies. And you start branching out from how things are done in your own company and your own experience, and you start learning from the experience of other people.

Joan emphasizes that the PAG structure often awakens the family business operators to the important issues of succession planning. "It's a place that introduced me to marriage contracts. I had never even thought about that in connecting with our business. One fellow told us that if we did not have a marriage contract in place when we marry, we could forfeit half of the shares in our company. He had learned from experience.

CHAPTER EIGHTEEN

PLANNING
FOR MANAGEMENT
SUCCESSION

Maybe it's because providing for an orderly management succession seems one thing the vigorous, busy young entrepreneur can safely put off until tomorrow. Maybe it's just unpleasant to contemplate one's own mortality or to face up to the disappointing lack of an obvious successor among one's associates or family members. Whatever the reason, planning for management succession is one of the issues that small business owners all too often neglect. It is a matter of "governance," to borrow the term used by Jonathan Kovacheff of Kovacheff Consulting Group Inc., to distinguish broad issues determining the overall constitution of a company from "operations," its practical day-to-day functioning. "Small businesses typically don't understand governance versus operation. And even in small business, there are many governance issues, mainly around stewarding the corporation and ensuring that it prospers."

Viewed from another perspective, succession planning might seem to be right up the entrepreneur's alley, involving as it does the ability to look into the future and chart a course towards a specific goal. In fact, my interviews included many interesting discussions of succession—for example, with Karen Flavelle, who recently succeeded her father as president of Purdy's Chocolates, and Joan Berta, president of CAFE, an association of family-run businesses. A number of the other entrepreneurs I talked with had had recent experiences in succession planning that did not involve family businesses. Their experiences, which we will look at next, should underscore the close connection between setting business goals, the everyday business of the entrepreneur, and succession planning, so that even the discussion here of the specifics of family-run businesses might yield valuable insights for every small business operator.

NON-FAMILY SUCCESSION

Succession planning isn't just something to be considered in the distant future when the currently youthful entrepreneur begins to consider retirement. Accident, illness, or family emergency might force anyone to make a radical change in their work tomorrow. Particularly for businesses run by entrepreneurs who keep everything in their own hands, the end is likely to follow the departure of the manager. If you are interested in seeing your business survive you, you have to consider getting a plan in place at once.

If you have time to plan, what should you be planning for? In the examples that follow, we will examine three cases of succession planning reported by the persons I interviewed for this book.

Case Study: Ensuring a Steady Supply of Good Managers

Human resources planning for continuity of personnel, including top managers, should be a priority for all companies. Look at the example of David Anderson and CANATOM NPM, which, because of the economic stagnation of the 1980s and the fact that they did not hire during that slump, has now found themselves facing issues related to replacing key personnel. David says the key human resources problem faced by the firm is the age of its workforce. "I would say the single most important HR issue facing us today is how do we bring in the talent required to ensure the continuity and, indeed, the growth of the company in the future."

He attributes the problem to "a profound growth period in the 1960s and through the 1970s, followed by stagnation in the 1980s. During that time, our company and others in the same field didn't bring in new blood because the levels of business were down." When sales picked up again in the later 1980s and early 1990s, customers overseas, especially in Korea, called on CANATOM NPM to supply trained plant personnel. "There was an overloading of experienced staff on those projects, and there were not significant opportunities to reduce the average age to rejuvenate the mix, to ensure continuity." The pressure to fill field positions with senior people has continued with CANATOM NPM's work on jobs outsourced by Ontario Hydro, but it has left the company with a shortage of junior people moving through on-the-job training.

CANATOM NPM is addressing the issue this way: "First of all, we go through an exercise roughly twice a year of identifying the key skill areas that have to be covered for the company to function. Who is the key resource for that particular skill area and who is the individual's back-up. What if that person were to be hit by a bus? So, to the extent that we have each of the key skill areas covered that the company has to have to service its client base, we have a minimum of a key resource and a back-up. The plan is that we don't fall below that minimum. And, actually, sometimes that has not been easy to do. We also look at it from the point of view that if these key resources are all nearing the end of their working life cycle, perhaps that plan is not adequate, and you need to have an heir apparent and a reserve for him or her. So we've done that."

David says that staff development is such an important priority that it has affected the way that CANATOM NPM bids for new jobs. "The other thing that we're doing is telling our clients that we want to work for them, we aren't going to say no to a staff augmentation role, but why don't they go a different way? Why don't they work out what it is they'd like us to do and have some sort of a risk/reward equation whereby we'll manage that task for them, or undertake to do it for a ceiling price with an incentive, or something like that. And when we do that, we then have a bit more flexibility as to which people we use. Obviously we still have to put experienced people on it, but maybe we can put a more-experienced with a less-experienced person, who in turn can become more experienced."

This example shows that succession must be managed for all significant positions in a company, not just the founder(s), owner(s), or senior manager(s). Staff must be rejuvenated, and methods and institutional memory should be passed along not only at the ownership and executive levels, but also on the supervisory, professional, and skilled levels.

Case Study: The Entrepreneur Who Wants to Go into Politics

David Haslam of Presidential Plumbing Ltd. is thinking of going into politics and is trying to arrange his company such that he could confidently step away from it and campaign. "If I was successful, I would naturally have to put my company in some sort of trust, and I would have to make sure that I had the appropriate people in place to look after my affairs. Right now, not only because of that, but I'm trying to have a large focus so that my company runs on its own so that I can more or less step aside and allow it to run. That's what my goal is over the next two years. My idea at the moment is to have a manager replace me. I'm not sure if that's the right way to go or whether I should merge with another company and they would have a vested interest in the company. It's a tough industry to be in."

David's approach might serve as a model for any entrepreneur: How would you secure a reliable successor if you wanted to step away from active management in order to pursue new interests? Would there be someone in-house already being groomed for promotion? Would you be able to find a manager with the necessary qualifications? Would you have to sell your business in order to maintain the value of your investment in the operation?

David's thoughtful and prudent approach to these questions yields several lessons. There are various ways to handle succession, each with its own difficulties and benefits. It may require a long period to determine which method is best for your business.

Once you have settled on a method, its implementation will be a continuing task. Succession must not be left to the last moment.

Case Study: The Founder Who Isn't Passing the Business along to Family

Kieran O'Briain says he has a vision for Kee Transport's long-term future, but that it does not involve handing down the business, which he founded, to his children. On the other hand, like David Haslam's plan for Presidential Plumbing Ltd., it does involve benefits for the founder/owner during his own lifetime. Kieran says that he took from his successful father the example of not thinking in terms of passing down a business within one's family. "My father didn't abandon me, but he also didn't leave a company for me to inherit either. I created this company on my own. It wasn't given to me. My father was there if I was ever in trouble. I knew he was there, but he didn't cut me a cheque and say, 'Here son, go open up your own business.' And nor will I do that for my kids.

"I was not spoiled in the literal sense, but I was in the sense that I knew he was there if I needed him. I would do much the same. I've always had the notion of growing this business enough that in ten years, when I hit about the age of 45, that I would elevate myself to the chairman of the board, and somebody working for me would become the president, then I would set up the corporate structure. By that point, the company would probably be pretty much already set up. I would probably have one vice-president and four or five managers. I'd have myself, a vice-president of operations, some kind of strong financial guy, and then the regions taking care of themselves. I just spent $50,000 to build myself an office in the basement of my house. I would stay home—not all the time, but I could travel when I wanted to, go to the regional offices, and do what I want. The company would have to be big enough to pay me and a president, so it has to be of a certain size to deal with that."

Kieran's remarks remind us that a founder/owner has the power to suit his or her beliefs and values when choosing a method of succession. Kieran has opted to seek and hire a president. It is also important to note that both he and David Haslam are planning succession with more in mind than simply having their companies continue after their deaths. They are creating ways by which the companies can continue while they leave the helm to pursue other interests, and yet it will still leave them the option to return or the ability to pick and choose their degree of involvement. A well-managed succession can enable an entrepreneur to change the way he or she participates in the business world to suit changing interests.

FAMILY SUCCESSION

We have all heard about the vitality of the small business sector, but even so, it may still come as a surprise to hear that there are more than one million family-owned businesses in Canada today. They generate more than 45 per cent of the gross domestic product and a pay cheque for about half of all working Canadians— that is, about 4.5 million people. Furthermore, 8 per cent of the new jobs created are coming from family businesses. How they will operate after the founders retire becomes a question for all Canadians, involving, as it does, such a large part of the economy. And the question is going to continue to be of special importance, according to Joan Berta, president of CAFE, as retiring baby boomers begin to pass on some $10 trillion in personal wealth to their heirs. Much of that wealth will reside in family-built business operations.

Joan provides another way to measure the potential impact on the economy of family businesses: "The statistics tell you that only three in ten businesses successfully get to the second generation. That doesn't mean that the other seven fail. It means that they're sold to another firm or to its employees and are not passed to the next generation of that family. But I would suggest that probably 20 or 30 per cent—two or three in ten—die. They either shut down, or if they do pass on to the next generation, they don't do so successfully, and a year or two down the road, the business will go under and be shut down anyway. And if 20 or 30 per cent of those businesses fail in the next 15 to 20 years, what's that going to do to our economy? It's a huge impact."

Jonathan Kovacheff adds, "The overwhelming majority of family-run businesses don't make it to the third generation because of family-related issues." These "family-related issues," in Kovacheff's term, will be met in the following sections of this chapter, and threaten orderly succession. They include:

• Splitting the business or giving it to unsuited persons out of the desire to be fair to children.

• Assuming that children will go into the business and hence failing to develop a program to familiarize them with it and develop their interest and skills.

• Not developing corporate culture, business plans, and job descriptions that family successors understand, agree to, and acquire training and competence for.

• Allowing family dynamics to control meetings and communications that are supposedly for business purposes.

• Succumbing to financial demands from family heirs that are bad for business.

Succession Problems: A Look at the United States?

A recent study conducted on family businesses in the United States shows that there, too, in a significant number of businesses about to change hands, little attention is being given to organizing succession. The project was sponsored by the Arthur Andersen Center for Family Business and the Mass-Mutual's Family Business Enterprise and was directed by Ross Nager, executive director of the Arthur Andersen Center. Why do so few family businesses develop succession and strategic plans? Nager says the answer lies in the conflict business founders have always faced between being a fair parent and being a sound businessperson. "As a parent, a founder wants to treat the children equally, which means dividing the wealth equally," he says. "But the businessperson knows that the business should go to the most capable, qualified candidate." Often the easiest solution is to ignore the conflict and not plan for the future.

In addition, leaders of family businesses can be reluctant to retire because their identity is so tied up with the business. As a result, they either put retirement off indefinitely or go into semi-retirement, creating an uncertain, unhealthy environment within the business. The real danger of this, says Nager, is that family-run businesses need strategic and succession planning even more than public businesses do for a number of reasons. First, CEOs of family businesses typically serve six times longer than their counterparts in public companies. That length of tenure makes the impact of change, when it comes, enormous. Second, family businesses have unique capital needs that require planning. For example, such businesses often must pay estate taxes when the founder dies. They must be prepared to buy out uninterested heirs. And the families can make unpredictable financial demands. "Exxon shareholders don't tell Exxon to pay a bigger dividend. Families do that all the time," says Nager. In the absence of articulated plans, family-owned companies are especially vulnerable to strategies that keep family members satisfied but may be bad for business.

While the survey raises concerns about the ability of family-run businesses to handle their inevitable transfers of power, some results suggest that these companies are becoming more sophisticated about other issues. For example, the families' wealth was more diversified than researchers had predicted. A majority of respondents reported that at least 40 per cent of their family's personal wealth is invested outside the family business. That diversification may make CEOs more likely to step down at regular retirement age because they feel more financially secure. In addition, heirs who are not running the company can inherit the outside assets, thus making it easier for founders to follow conventional advice. This is what Nager calls "pruning the tree"—leaving the stock only to the heirs who will run the business. This evidence of increasing financial sophistication is reassuring, says Nager.

Three Barriers to Successful Transition

The study identified three significant problems:

• Lack of Strategic Planning

• Plans for Co-CEOs

• Weak Boards

Lack of Strategic Planning: More than two-thirds of the companies surveyed have no written strategic plan. "Often the CEO has a picture in his own mind of what will happen next," says Ross Nager, director of the research project and executive director of the Arthur Andersen Center for Family Business. "If that's as far as it goes, the firm faces a serious problem if poor health forces him to retire or if he dies in office."

A written strategic plan is an element of "governance," as mentioned earlier. Like a country, a firm that intends to continue through the generations requires something like a constitution, which consists of unwritten elements (for instance, institutional memory of practices and procedures) and written elements, including strategic planning documents that define targeted business sectors, achievement goals, and the like. Strategic plans and goals may be obvious to the founder/owner, but if he or she dies, their plans may die too unless they are formulated in a written document that has been developed in consultation with other key company members and with successors.

Plans for Co-CEOs: Forty-two per cent of the respondents reported that two or more family members may serve as co-CEOs in the next generation. Nager calls that a "notoriously fragile and difficult way to run a company."

It is likely that in many cases, plans for family co-CEO successors result from reluctance to choose among family members, fear of provoking arguments, or the desire to please everyone. In other words, such plans are not really ways of creating a sensible succession plan but of avoiding the problems involved, and they spring from the "family-related issues" mentioned above. Anyone who wants to know what is likely to result from co-CEOs should just think back to his or her high school study of Shakespeare's *Julius Caesar*.

Weak Boards: Less than half the boards of directors meet more than twice a year, the research showed, and more than two-thirds are not paid. These statistics suggest that family businesses are not building and using strong boards even though many will be called on to play a strong role when leadership changes hands.

Of course, succession does not have to be handled or facilitated by a board, and some small businesses may not even have one, depending on the nature of the organizaiton and the preferences of the founder. But where the board is charged with a major role in succession, a weak board is unlikely to have either the commitment or the competence to direct a transition, monitor the successor's success, and redirect or replace the successor if necessary.

Case Studies: Two Canadian Stories of Succession

The remainder of this chapter will present in some detail two different perspectives on the problem of family business succession in Canada. The first is Joan Berta's, which combines her own family business experience and her years of work with CAFE, an association of family businesses of which she is currently the president. The second is Karen Flavelle's, who recently succeeded her father as president of Purdy's Chocolates. Both Joan and Karen provide a valuable corrective to the worries we have been bringing forward so far, in the successful methods they have found for securing family business succession.

> ### SECRETS OF SUCCESS IN SUCCESSION PLANNING
> - Start planning early.
> - Think of the family business as an asset, not just an operation.
> - Let family members have a free choice on whether or not to enter the business.
> - Get professional help for the transition process.

Joan had a few words of insight of special value: "One of the biggest issues you have to overcome is, number one, everyone's problems are unique. And number two, they don't want anybody to know that the family isn't getting along. You have this wonderful, successful business and everything is smiley-face and isn't this wonderful, but then the door closes and the screaming and throwing starts." And yet, she emphasized, the importance of family businesses to those operating them and to the national economy underscores the importance of finding ways to get the problems out in the open and solved effectively.

Joan Berta and CAFE

Joan Berta was not a founding member of the Canadian Association of Family Enterprises (CAFE). She explains, "CAFE was formed in 1984 as an association of family members by a number of large firms to address the issues of family-owned enterprises in which at least one or more family members work in the organization. It was started by the likes of Bata Shoes, Tilden Rent-a-Car, E.D.Smith, Sharwood, a mid-level banker, and other very well-known companies in Canada today. Morrison Lamothe, up in Ottawa, was involved very early, and, I think, Pioneer Petroleum. They realized they had a unique situation, and they were looking for people to share it with. Finally, 14 families got together and incorporated CAFE, and it grew from there."

Joan sees CAFE as a very successful response to some of the basic needs of the family business operator. "Often, the founder has got this thriving business, and he's never thought of what he will do, how he will retire, because he's the technician, and most of these people who are the technicians don't see their business as an asset. They don't see it as an asset to be managed, and so long as we can put the right management structure in place and know how to manage money, we have a business. And that's really what CAFE is intending to do. CAFE is trying to help these people understand the resource that they really have, manage that resource, and manage it through succession. And that's the tough one: managing it through succession."

Managing through succession has to start early. "Success is very much about starting to plan early because a lot of people really do not do that. It is extremely important to begin to sort out whether your children are interested in the business. We have a program that we call family councils, and we advocate that every family meet quarterly, at the least half-yearly, with all the family members, active in the business or not. You can do it around the kitchen table or more formally, and you should have a facilitator so it's not just the owner of the business barking at everybody. But start talking about the business, what it is, its culture, what it does, where it finds its customers, how it has thrived and survived. In this way, the children, from a young age, start getting a sense and feeling of the business, what it means to the family, and whether or not they might want to be a part of it.

"We're long past the time when your name was Smith because you were a blacksmith and your son was a blacksmith and your daughter married a blacksmith. There's a lot more choices in terms of careers for the generations growing up today. So it's important to establish very early with your children—your nieces and nephews, or whoever—whether or not they're interested in going into the business."

Encouraging children to find their own path means the company must also find its own way. It is vital, according to Joan, for companies to consider whether or not family members are, in fact, equipped to take over management. "A lot of the businesses, particularly the smaller ones, don't think about the suitability of the person to the position. 'That's my son and/or daughter, so automatically they're going to come into the business.' But they may not have the skills, there's no job description in place, and there's no clear rules. Till their dying day, Father or Mother call the shots, tell everybody what they have to do, and a lot of frustration and animosity can build up with the kids. And as a result, succession is not successful, if it happens at all."

Animosity can also come from a lack of honesty. Joan provides an example of a company whose succession problems have led to its disappearance as a family business: "There were two generations working in this family. There were four kids working in the business, and they were all doing a pretty good job. The parents individually told each one of the kids that they were going to take over the business because they didn't have the courage to pick a successor. When the parents retired, all four kids stepped up, thinking they were taking over, and then the fighting began. Eventually the father sold the business, but the family relations remained very strained."

Joan emphasizes that hiring a professional manager can be an ideal solution for a founder struggling with a seeming lack of alternatives for succession. She says that the companies that make such an arrangement "are the ones that started the planning early and recognized the value of doing that; you can put a structure in place with professional management." Her own family business has a contingency plan for emergencies, which incorporates the hiring of an interim professional manager to give the children time to decide how to proceed. "If anything should happen to my husband and me simultaneously, we have three people who will manage this company for a year until our children determine what they want to do."

Karen Flavelle and Purdy's Chocolates

Karen Flavelle describes the succession process that brought her to the presidency of Purdy's last year. She is the only one of three children who had any interest in business. "My two siblings didn't want to live in a city, let alone work in a business, whereas I did a B.Com. and have always been interested in business. We grew up understanding that the business was going to be sold when Mom and Dad retired. We didn't think of it as a family business. It was Dad's thing, so it wasn't part of my program. As I went through my career, it just happened to be a coincidence that I liked business, so I went into packaged goods marketing, and back in those early days of my career, my goal was to be vice-president of a big packaged goods company.

"Then we all started to think it would be a shame to just sell this business. We began to think that maybe we should keep it. And at that point, I was thinking of it more like a family home and the emotional attachment of having grown up with it and all of that. And so I proposed to the family that we keep the business but have it run by professional managers when Dad didn't want to do it anymore, and they liked that idea. Then we all started to think, it doesn't work very well having professional managers."

Then Karen's professional goals began to change. "Part of what I was looking for was to get out of packaged goods because I could just see the balance of power shifting from packaged goods to retail. I liked being where the control was, so after I did this assessment, I decided that a smaller retail company seemed to fit my strengths and weaknesses. I headed into retail, initially in Toronto.

"Dad's memory about not selling the company is a little bit different from mine. He recalls that in the beginning, he thought he was never going to die, but then he started to realize that he probably wasn't going to be around forever. Employees began asking what's going to happen with the company, and that, combined with my interest in becoming involved in the company, all started to make sense. Originally he had been resistant to parachuting an offspring in on top of all these people who'd been there for so long.

"He saw me working on the lines in the plant for a year, and that wasn't where I saw myself. So we worked through that for a while because I refused to move my husband and family out to an uncertain situation. I had to know how fast the transition to presidency would be. So, we did all our negotiation long distance until we were both comfortable and we had the same expectations. Through the process, I realized that he couldn't guarantee that I would become president because I still had to prove myself, but I wanted to make sure we both agreed that the plan was for me to prove myself and become president in two to three years."

Karen entered the company in the position of executive vice-president and at once began a four-month orientation that involved visits to all 42 Purdy's stores and a week in the factory performing a variety of jobs. "My first specific responsibility was to run the retail side of the business, and I focused primarily on merchandising, marketing, and store design. I then got more involved in retail operations."

The expanding responsibilities she took on as executive vice-president extended into marketing, finance, and manufacturing. She became president a little more than a year ago. "You know, you just take on more and more, do more and more, and then delegate other things so you have time to take on more things. So, it wasn't like all of a sudden I was president. I was already doing the job." One day Dad said, "You know, you're doing everything that I ever did as president. Did you know that?" I hadn't realized it. She added, "Well, I'm awfully lucky with my father because it's quite amazing how receptive he is to ideas, how willing to change things that have been done certain ways. I guess it's because of his strong belief in consensus decision making."

The human resources responsibilities took up an increasingly important part of her role. "I had an expectation that I would come in and, because Purdy's had a great team already and everything was working the way it should be, that everything would just continue the way it was. However, I found that I had to change the teams and the personnel around in order to ensure that the vision was achieved." Karen, who had worked with one of CAFE's personal advisory groups throughout the transition, learned in consultation with her group that such personnel changes often occur as part of management transition. Reassured, she went on to receive the heartening message from her father that he was pleased with her performance.

The worry that remains is whether she will be able to balance the demands of the business with her commitment to her own young children—an eight-, five-, and a four-year-old. "I'm not willing to sacrifice my life just to grow the business. So, I'm really concentrating more on building the bench strengths. The growth opportunities aren't clear. They may be for some businesses, but I don't think they are for us because we're in every big mall in British Columbia and Alberta that we want to be in. So there's incremental things that we can do to build our strength and our volume, but the leap would be something like moving to Ontario. I'm not prepared to make that sacrifice to my family."

Karen ended with some excellent pieces of advice:

- Work outside the company for a long time before entering your family's business.
- Don't bring your kids up with the idea that they're going into the family business.
- Use a mediator during the transition of succession.

HIRING A CONSULTANT

This do-it-yourself guide to human resources would not be complete without addressing the issue of when and how to hire a consultant. Whether the idea comes with a particular project—like doing a marketing study—or with the prospect of a wide-ranging reorganization following a change of leadership, most small business operators at one time or another have considered hiring some temporary outside help.

They may look enviously at their larger competitors who seem to benefit effortlessly from consultants. According to Jonathan Kovacheff of Kovacheff Consulting Group Inc., larger businesses do indeed have important strategic advantages over small and medium-size ones when dealing with consultants. "Larger businesses have at least two added advantages. One is that they have a lot of in-house people whom they can access for certain types of expertise, and the second advantage is that they use consultants more and know how to manage them, which is a trick in itself. So small businesses are at a disadvantage in both of these areas. They don't have the in-house expertise, and they don't have the longer-term understanding of how to manage a consultant."

Another disadvantage for many small businesses seeking expert help, Jonathan says, is that "they don't have the network to be able to access the right consultants." And yet small businesses often have as great a need to hire the services of an outside expert for a limited time.

> In this chapter, we will consider three issues:
>
> • How You Know if You Need a Consultant
>
> • How to Find a Consultant
>
> • Getting Value for Your Money

In our consideration of hiring a consultant, we will be guided by three experts: Jonathan Kovacheff of Kovacheff Consulting Group Inc., Joan Berta of CAFE, and Lynda Bowles of Deloitte and Touche. In addition, we have information about consulting from a number of the entrepreneurs interviewed. David Anderson of CANATOM NPM, Karen Flavelle of Purdy's Chocolates, and Susan Niczowski of Summer Fresh Salads Inc. have all worked with consultants and provided details of what worked and what didn't. Others, including David Haslam of Presidential Plumbing Ltd., have yet to contract work out to a professional consultant: "I have not really used consultants," he told me, "for any part of my business. I have found that the best consultant really is myself. Keeping your ears open and taking little bits and pieces of advice from other people are what make me successful."

HOW YOU KNOW IF YOU NEED A CONSULTANT

Jonathan Kovacheff identifies four areas in which consultants can help a small business operator:

• expertise in identifying problems

• expertise in solving problems

• facilitation skills

• implementation help

About expertise, he says, "They bring something to the table that you can't get internally, and in most small businesses, that's going to be in a variety of areas just because of cost problems and the fact that you can't have a large infrastructure." Jonathan defines facilitation skills, the third reason for getting a consultant, as "the ability to actually get groups together and work through problems." The fourth reason, implementation help, he calls a combination of the others, moving from ideas and getting agreement to building "structures for implementation that help the client actually drive the conclusion."

Thus, deciding that you need a consultant is a process with four stages: recognizing that you have a problem, recognizing that you do not have the expertise to define and solve it, recognizing that your company does not have this expertise internally, and recognizing that the problem must be defined and dealt with by bringing in outside expertise. At that point, Jonathan comments, the entrepreneur must ask, "How do I actually access the networks that will fulfil a need that I know I have? Many times, it's a problem for even large organizations to know what the need is. Smaller organizations with no experience just know they have a problem, but they don't know whether it's structural, an HR problem, or an operational one. Thus, they need to access a network to just figure out what the problem is and then get the right person to help them address the problem. They also need to find people who will work for less, often half of what a large organization can pay; that makes them very difficult to find."

Certain Tasks Require Expertise

The entrepreneurs interviewed identified a number of areas in which they had used consultants, and many of them related specifically to human resources. "We've used some consulting firms and basically, we've used them for various aspects of the business, whether it's looking at our efficiency rates or how we can improve our productivity," Susan Niczowski says.

David Anderson's experience at CANATOM NPM is more wide ranging. "We have used consultants in a number of areas. We have used them to help do market surveys to help us decide whether we should go into certain new areas or not. Rather than have somebody from inside who is not knowledgeable in that particular area, we've hired somebody to do that for us on occasion. We've hired consultants to help us with our strategic planning, to coach in presentation skills, and to help some of the team create out-of-the-box thinking with respect to how to create distinctive value in our product, how can we differenti-ate our service from that of others."

Lynda Bowles considers consultants particularly helpful in the human resources functions such as employee hiring. "I've seen companies hiring staff, and they don't have the skills to do it and end up hiring the wrong people. There are huge costs associated with improper hiring, including severance costs and the prob-lems that may have been caused in the firm. They would have been better off if they had used a professional at the begining, one who would have weeded out incompatible applicants." She goes on, "I think there are some skills, such as knowing person-alities and how they work together, that require the use of a pro-fessional consultant."

HOW TO FIND A CONSULTANT

Jonathan Kovacheff sees a common pattern in looking for a con-sultant, and it is not always the best pattern. "From my experi-ence, what generally happens is that the individual asks whomever they're closest to: their banker, lawyer, accountant, or other busi-ness people. They might belong to an association and ask them whom they would recommend. This obviously is a powerful tool, but it also can be a limited one because the body of help that is out there is quite large now, but it's not an easily accessible group. Your family lawyer might know one or two people, but that may not be what you need."

Joan Berta finds CAFE, particularly its personal advisory groups (described at greater length in Chapter 17), a very help-ful source of consultant candidates. "Certainly within CAFE, we use our PAGs to talk about consultants somebody else has used or whom they know." She recommends a wide range of other sources as well. "You can go to your local chamber of com-merce or board of trade. They know these people. Certainly you can come to CAFE, and we can identify them for you. You can go to the Canadian Society of Association Executives since they will know all the different associations. And, depending on what you need a consultant for—whether it's an overall business consultant or if it's financial management or whatever—I would really recommend going to a professional association to find your consultants."

Screening The Candidates

Referrals are a good first step, says Susan Niczowski, but there's more involved in the search for a consultant than just accepting a suggestion. According to Susan, her company has "basically shopped around and tried to deal with people with whom we've dealt in the past, people who we know. Again, coming from a large organization and knowing a lot of people in the food industry, that kind of eliminates a lot of the errors. And basically, you ask around and get referrals, and then you sit down and see what they can do. We've had some consultants referred, and they haven't worked for us because they just weren't suitable. You live and learn."

Jonathan Kovacheff suggests a broad search followed by personal interviews with leading candidates. "I would say that probably the best way to do this is to go to as many sources as possible and get referrals, then arrange an interview and spend quite a bit of up-front time with potential consultants. You need to tell them what you think you need, what you do, how you would approach it, what your cost structure is. You must do all these things, especially if it's the first time you're using a consultant."

He goes on, "Many businesses end up using their accounting firm that has an entrepreneurial or small business consultant attached to them. And that can be both good and bad. Costs are somewhat higher and you always wonder about the relationship of someone who is not only a financial adviser or auditor but is also selling consulting work. I'm not attacking the quality of the consulting; it's just a question of how much independence and how much control you actually have. But going with the accounting-consulting firm would be the route taken by most businesses."

Commenting on the same issue, Lynda Bowles suggested, "Only contract out those specific pieces that require the high level of expertise. You don't need a major firm doing your bookkeeping for you, for example."

Ask for Proposals

Even the best consultant will not be useful to your company unless you do two things: give the consultant a clear and complete description of the task you want performed, and obtain from the consultant a detailed proposal of services including a comprehensive estimate of costs. Dissatisfaction with a consultant often springs from failure to establish these two basics of good communications. If your company and the consultant have different ideas about the task involved, you are likely to find yourself feeling overbilled and underserved. And you'll be right…but it may not be the consultant's fault; it may be yours.

Small business operators should ask prospective consultants for a detailed proposal of services. Lynda Bowles says: "I was at someone's place last week, and they were complaining about the consultant they had hired to help them do their business plan. The firm had quoted a fee, but before the project was complete, they announced that the fee had "expired" and they needed to renegotiate the amount. They tried another consulting firm and finally ended up doing the business plan themselves. They did not feel that the consultants had really helped. There is fault on both sides, but I don't think the entrepreneur knew what they were buying."

Lynda provided another example. "I had another client who told me that they had done the business plan and all they needed me to do was to put the "finishing touches" on it. Well, the plan was a disaster! None of the financial models worked, and the original plan did not explain the potential of the company for prospective lenders. So we had to rewrite the plan from scratch. A lot has to do with understanding what you are contracting for."

It comes down again to the entrepreneur's responsibility for developing and monitoring company strategy. According to Lynda, "I think it's important that you understand what it is that you want to buy and know what it is that you're actually getting. You can't give that away to somebody else or it never works."

Lynda recommends getting two or three quotes on a job. "If you find that one quote is way out of whack, you have to wonder why. Did they see something that the others missed? Because of this, you really must review the proposal critically. I think you've got to assume that all firms are basically the same, and everybody wants the job. Be aware of the firms that make promises but don't keep them. Don't be misled. The firm that was really honest and didn't make the promises they knew they couldn't keep may have been bypassed in favour of the firm that promised you the moon but didn't deliver."

Checking Out Consultants

The best way to identify the trustworthy consultant or consulting firm is to have your own clear definition of what you want. This will enable you to judge which proposal(s) are realistic and complete and use methods that are likely to accomplish your goal.

The experts I interviewed recommended asking consultants for references and taking the time to check them. Of course, any consultant's list of clients and accomplishments will be designed to put him or her in a favourable light. But a reference check can do more than just verify the consultant's stated experience if you ask the right questions. If possible, talk to former clients whose businesses are similar to your own. Ask for specifics:

- Exactly what was asked of the consultant and in what time frame?

- Did the consultant accomplish the task within the contracted period?

- Did the consultant provide and adhere to a proposal of services and an estimate of costs?

- Was the consultancy a positive experience for people within the company who had to deal with the consultant?

- Has the former client experienced the value added to his or her business that was envisioned when the hiring of a consultant was first planned?

- Would the former client hire the consultant again?

Similarly, ask specific questions when interviewing the consultant. It is hard to say in advance what these specifics should be because they depend upon the task you want done. Since you will probably wish to interview serious prospects more than twice, you could think in terms of conducting your interviews by moving towards questions that are as specific as you can make them. Interview first for initial information about the consultant;

provide the consultant with your definition of the task. Interview the second time to ask more specific questions resulting from your reference checks and analysis of the consultant's qualifications; receive the consultant's detailed proposal and estimate. Interview the third time to ask specific questions emerging from the consultant's proposal and estimate.

Does the Consultant Fit In with Your Culture

One of the main things you're trying to discover is whether or not the consultant will fit in with your company culture. The entrepreneur should look for someone who is comfortable to work with; both the small business operators and the experts I interviewed agreed on this point. Speaking of her years as an entrepreneur before joining the staff of CAFE, Joan Berta said of choosing a consultant, "It is something like picking your doctor. There has to be a fit."

Jonathan Kovacheff agrees. "You have to feel comfortable with the individual. I've seen many technically very competent consultants blow up and not deliver value because they just didn't know how to work with a particular style. There has to be a fit."

Lynda Bowles recommends interviewing at least a few candidates, looking for a good personality fit. "You've got to be able to get along with them. A lot of it is personality. When you're an entrepreneur, you want somebody to be interested in what it is you're doing, and you want them to anticipate what your needs are."

In the foregoing sections, methods were recommended for ensuring the consultant you hire is competent. It is equally important that he or she be compatible. If you are hiring a consulting firm, it is vital to be compatible with the members of the firm you will actually be working with, and you should insist that it is they who are primarily involved in your interviewing process. This is not a simple task, and you must rely on your own insight and care to see you through. On the one hand, you don't want to hire a consultant because you like the person and are reasonably impressed with his or her self-presentation, only to discover incompetence, lack of thoroughness, or other shortcomings later. On the other hand, you don't want to screen so carefully for expertise and probity that you fail to notice until too late that the consultant is not really interested in your company, does not sympathize with your goals and your people, offends important employees, or is just personally grating to you.

When to Go with a Big Firm

At times, a small company, and even a start-up, may want to hire a large consulting firm for such matters as information technology or financial arrangements for a business that will have national or international ties. These are areas in which large firms in management consulting, financial consulting, technology or engineering consulting, and other such fields often possess expertise otherwise unavailable.

A small company may feel it is unable to afford the services of large consultants, but in many cases, the big firms are willing to provide advice at a discounted rate for small businesses that seem stable, well-grounded, and likely to grow. Therefore, it is possible that a large consultant is an option for you.

Lynda Bowles of Deloitte and Touche is drawing on her knowledge of that giant among consultants when she gives the following advice about start-up firms approaching large consultants: "There may be different stages when you need a financial consultant. For instance, in the start-up stages, you may think that you can't afford to go to a big firm. But on the other hand, maybe you can't afford *not* to go to a big firm because there are some decisions that have to be made at the start-up stage that can have a big impact on the future, especially if you're in the information technology area. It could have an adverse effect for the business down the line. A lot of the major firms will make an investment in a small business if they see the potential for growth. And what the firm wants to do is grow with you."

She goes on, "Yes, if the consultant sees that the firm has growth potential, they want to grow with them. That's how we all make money, when everybody grows. So in some cases, the firm would be willing to make an investment themselves to help the company get on their way, knowing that down the road, they are going to benefit from that investment. And they will help the company. But it gets to be a decision as to whether they believe in the honesty of the entrepreneur and whether the entrepreneur really does try to commit to their part of the relationship."

GETTING VALUE FOR YOUR MONEY

Once a consultant is selected, the small business operator should not proceed without a signed contract specifying the work to be done, the timetable for the work, the fee structure, and penalties if the work is not satisfactory. According to Jonathan Kovacheff, "The best way to ensure the quality of service in consulting is the way one would ensure it with anything. First, contract hard by telling them of your perceived need and asking them to either submit a proposal or engagement letter that lays out their understanding of your needs. They also need to outline how they are going to approach that problem, what you can expect at the end of that contract, and exactly what each chunk of it is going to cost and why."

How Much Should You Pay?

David Anderson, who has had extensive experience in hiring consultants for CANATOM NPM, provided me with an overview of ways and means for setting pay scales for consultants. "How do we know how much to pay them? Well, in some cases, you have some knowledge of the going rate in the market, and in others, we might in fact have invited proposals from more than one consultant to give us an idea of how much the project should cost. But my general approach to negotiating the consulting fees is to bargain them down. No matter what amount is mentioned, I always flinch and say that we could never be able to go as high as that. In some cases, the reaction, quite rightly, is that that is their rate, take it or leave it. In other cases, they say that they'd really like to work for you and that they could do a little better than that. And so I'll flinch again, and say that it's still a lot more than we had in mind. After negotiating back and forth, there will come a point when they say that that's the very best they can do. That's when you offer 10 per cent less. If they take it, then you know what the real bottom line was."

"The quickest way to find out what things are costing in the market is to get two or three quotes." Jonathan Kovacheff suggests, "If you go to just one supplier, you never know if it's in a specific range, especially if you have absolutely no experience in how much something costs."

Measuring Value Received

Jonathan Kovacheff provided me with another helpful way for the entrepreneur to assess the value of a consultant's services and, at the same time, set a price for them. "The other thing that you look at is what the expected return should be, even if it's not measurable. If you spend $20,000 on X, it should be giving you something in the long run: either reducing conflict, increasing effectiveness, or operational efficiencies. In some kinds of consulting, that's much easier to measure. For instance, in a situation in which you're implementing technology, there's enough data on it so that you can actually say we expect it to reduce your overall costs by X per cent per year.

"Interventions such as change management assessment, leadership assessment, and governance work have benefits that are more intangible and less direct. However, one should still see and feel the benefits in reduced conflict, increased discussion, increased effectiveness of decision making, better working relations, or better quality of technical skills in your management. "So, define the end state first, and then look at how you can actually get value and how you would measure the value. Even if it's a qualitative measurement, make sure you know what it is. Like reduced conflict, for example."

Joan Berta concurs. "We pay our family councils facilitator US$1,350 a day, and we have two-day meetings about three or four times a year. It's an expensive process, but compared to the posssible loss of the business, it is a drop in the bucket."

Satisfaction Must Be Guaranteed

One final point on paying for consulting help was emphasized by Jonathan Kovacheff. "Make sure you both understand what the consultant will be paid for, and ensure that payment happens only if what is requested is delivered."

Communications with the consultant doesn't end with signing the contract, Lynda Bowles emphasizes; the entrepreneur needs to stay in regular contact. "You should actually be overseeing the consultant as they're going along. Keep in touch with them. Have regular reporting meetings, and write that into the contract. Otherwise, they end up going off on tangents and try to charge you for work you may not have wanted or needed. And then it gets to be an adversarial relationship, which isn't what you want to have."

A related suggestion comes from Jonathan Kovacheff: contract for consulting work in phases. That way, if something should prove unsatisfactory, the problem is limited, and there is an opportunity for a non-adversarial end to the relationship. "Ensure that you determine the phases and deliverables of the consulting assignment. This way, you can end the relationship after the first phase if the required deliverables do not materialize."

Jonathan and Lynda emphasize that only you guarantee your own satisfaction by carefully controlling your relationship with a consultant. Develop a list of possible consultants through reliable sources such as business acquaintances and professional associations. Interview hard: ask specific questions and look for not only competence but also compatibility with your business. Demand a detailed proposal of services and cost estimate. Make this the basis of a contract that guarantees your satisfaction by defining what is to be accomplished and provides for payment upon receipt. To further guarantee your satisfaction, contract for consulting services in phases so that in effect, you make performance reviews along the way and can terminate an unproductive relationship before it goes too far. Finally, keep in touch with the consultant and his or her work as it progresses: oversee what is being done and what you are likely to receive.

FOOTNOTES

Chapter 1

[1]Allan Riding and Barbara Orser, *Beyond the Banks: Creative Financing for Canadian Entrepreneurs* (Toronto: John Wiley & Sons Canada, Ltd, 1998) p.32.

[2]Joanne Thomas Yaccato and Paula Juberville, *Raising Your Business: A Canadian Woman's Guide to Entrepreneurs* (Toronto: Prentice-Hall Canada Inc., 1998) p.55.

[3]Royal Trust poll cited by Elaine Carey in "Your Business," *The Toronto Star* (15 October 1998) p.88.

[4]*Your Business Matters: Starting Out Right* (Toronto: Royal Bank of Canada, 1990).

[5]Rick Spence, *Secrets of Success from Canada's Fastest-Growing Companies* (Toronto: John Wiley & Sons Canada, Ltd, 1998).

Chapter 2

[1]Rick Spence, *Secrets of Success from Canada's Fastest-Growing Companies* (Toronto: John Wiley & Sons Canada, Ltd, 1998).

[2]*Ibid.p.200.*

Chapter 3

[1]"Hire Stronger Faster," PROFIT (April/May 1998) p.44.

[2]*The Definitive Guide to Managing Human Resources for Small Business Owners* (Toronto: Royal Bank of Canada, 1998) p.4.

[3]"Hire Stronger Faster," p.44.

[4]*Ibid.*

[5]*Ibid.*

Chapter 5

[1]*The Definitive Guide to Managing Human Resources for Small Business Owners* (Toronto: Royal Bank of Canada, 1998) p.8.

[2]Margaret Kerr and JoAnn Kurtz, *Make It Legal: What Every Canadian Entrepreneur Needs to Know about the Law* (Toronto: John Wiley & Sons Canada, Ltd, 1998) p.197.

Chapter 6

[1]"Hire Stronger Faster," PROFIT (April/May 1998) p.46.

Chapter 9

[1]*The Definitive Guide to Managing Human Resources for Small Business Owners* (Toronto: Royal Bank of Canada, 1998) p.1.

[2]*The Definitive Guide to Managing Human Resources for Small Business Owners* (Toronto: Royal Bank of Canada, 1998).

Chapter 13

[1]For more on SMART goal setting, see comments by David Anderson, cited in Chapter 1.

Chapter 14

[1]Rick Spence, *Secrets of Success from Canada's Fastest-Growing Companies* (Toronto: John Wiley & Sons Canada, Ltd, 1998) 198.

[2]Spence, pp.203–204.

Chapter 16

[1]Margaret Kerr and JoAnn Kurtz, *Make It Legal: What Every Canadian Entrepreneur Needs to Know about the Law* (Toronto: John Wiley & Sons Canada, Ltd, 1997) p.229.

[2]Rick Spence, *Secrets of Success from Canada's Fastest-Growing Companies* (Toronto: John Wiley & Sons Canada, Ltd, 1998) p.208.

[3]Kerr and Kurtz, p.222.

[4]*Ibid.*

Chapter 17

[1]Larry Ginsberg, "Behind Every Great Entrepreneur Is a Great Team," *The Globe and Mail* (14 Sept. 1998) p.B11.

INDEX